UNDERSTANDING
YOUR PERSONAL
PROPHECY

UNDERSTANDING
YOUR PERSONAL
PROPHECY

How to Evaluate, Judge, Interpret,
and Apply Personal Prophecy

GARY G. CAKE

DESTINY IMAGE® PUBLISHERS, INC.

P.O. Box 310, Shippensburg, PA 17257-0310

"Speaking to the Purposes of God for this Generation and for the Generations to Come."

This book and all other Destiny Image, Revival Press, Mercy Place,

Fresh Bread, Destiny Image Fiction, and Treasure House books are available at Christian bookstores and distributors worldwide.

For a U.S. bookstore nearest you, call 1-800-722-6774.

For more information on foreign distributors, call 717-532-3040.

Reach us on the Internet: www.destinyimage.com.

ISBN 10: 0-7684-2589-1
ISBN 13: 978-0-7684-2589-5

For Worldwide Distribution, Printed in the U.S.A.

1 2 3 4 5 6 7 8 9 10 11 / 11 10 09 08

DEDICATION

This book is dedicated to my family—my wife, Sandy, our daughter, Charlene, and our son, Patterson. They lived with me while I learned all the lessons that made this book possible. Sandy believed in me during dark days when I might have given up if not for her faith in me. She and Patterson encouraged me to write this book and proofed it over and over until we were all satisfied. Thanks for putting up with me as I struggled to learn these truths and to put them on paper.

ENDORSEMENTS

Understanding Your Personal Prophecy: How to Evaluate, Judge, Interpret, and Apply Personal Prophecy has some unique approaches the understanding of how God speaks. Gary Cake addresses the way that we can evaluate both subjective and objective revelation that is coming into our lives. I especially enjoy the analysis that he makes about the buoys that made passage safe for his father-in-law's boat. He correlates those eight buoys to eight key guiding principles to help you make safe passage through your life with the revelation God is giving you. I am a warrior, so I love how Gary encourages us to mix the Word of God with faith to see full manifestation of His will in our life.

DR. CHUCK D. PIERCE
Glory of Zion International Ministries, Inc.

Gary Cake has done all of us who value both the gift of prophecy and the office of the prophet an enormous service. *Understanding Your Personal Prophecy* is, without a doubt, the best-written and clearest guideline to properly handling personal prophecies I have read. Thirty years in the "cooking processing" of God has given Gary both authenticity and profound insight into the value and realm of personal prophetic guidance and vision.

DENNIS PEACOCKE
President, Strategic Christian Services
Founder, Kingdom Ministries International

What a powerful time we are living in! God is releasing fresh words from His throne. The problem is that many people do not understand how to embrace and receive the full benefit of these words. Gary Cake takes the mystery out of the prophetic and makes it amazingly practical in his book, *Understanding Your Personal Prophecy*. Cake helps believers prepare themselves for success by providing guidelines for giving and receiving prophetic ministry. He brings wisdom by correcting some of the mistakes made in the past and revealing an excellent way for releasing prophecy. I highly recommend this book for anyone desiring to shift to a new level in prophetic ministry!

BARBARA WENTROBLE
Founder, International Breakthrough Ministries
Author, *Prophetic Intercession*; *Praying With Authority*;
You Are Anointed; *Rise to Your Destiny, Woman of God*

CONTENTS

PREFACE

Many years ago, a friend invited me to attend the church he pastored because a prophet was coming to minister and my friend knew of my interest in prophecy. Naturally, people were sitting on the edge of their seats hoping that they would receive a prophecy that evening. We all knew that there would not be time for everyone to receive that ministry. It turned out to be sort of an embarrassing evening for me. During the course of the meeting, the man called me up for ministry three times. Here was a roomful of people hoping to get one chance at receiving a prophecy and I, a guest, got three.

The combination of the prophecies given to me that night turned out to be rather complex. Part of it was really consistent with things already in my life. The man "read my mail," as we sometimes refer to these experiences. I could readily agree with that part. Part of it related to hopes I had for the future. I really liked that part. Part of it was very difficult. It challenged some of my preconceptions about how God would do things in my life. I did not understand it, but instinctively I knew it was true. (This prophecy will be discussed more in Chapter 8 as an illustration.)

Years later, after God had taken me through all the training that the prophecy had alluded to, two of my mentors prophesied to me in the exact wording of the first prophecy that the training was near completion. I was so excited! As I was riding home from the meeting, I said to God, "If this is almost over, how can I cooperate with you to expedite the completion of this?" As clearly as I have ever heard God, he spoke to me internally and said, "Repent!" Now I have figured out over the years that there is no point in pretending when talking to God. I am just honest with him. He already knows what is going on inside of me. At that moment, I really did not have a clue what I needed to repent for. So I asked, "For what?" He began to show me how I had failed to cooperate with that prophecy from years ago, and how I had resisted what he had been doing in my life for all of these years. It simply did not fit my paradigm of how God operated, so I had struggled with it. As God showed me what had gone on over the last 15 years, my life history began to fall in place and I saw it in a way I never had seen it before. I repented! In fact I think I cried for about two weeks.

No one I had asked for help over all those years knew how to advise me regarding that prophecy. I could find no book that addressed how I was supposed to respond to a prophecy filled with such a mixture. I walked this prophecy through by trial and error (if you read my dedication, you will understand it better after reading this). I made it! But could it have been easier? Could the process have been shortened? I am positive the first question could be answered in the affirmative; probably not the second one.

When I think of the verse where Jesus told Saul (Paul) how hard it was to "kick against the goads" (Acts 26:14), I get a picture of a weed that grew in the fields where I grew up. I have never bothered to look up what a goad really is because the picture of this weed seems sufficient. We called it loco weed. It had large seedpods covered with sharp points. They were not thistles or even stickers, just long, stiff, spike-like prongs. When they dried, they were very sharp. Our job as kids was to pull these up in the field. One time, we got the idea to throw these pods at one another. What a fight we had— until my dad discovered we were spreading seedpods all over the field. We only did that once!

When I think of kicking the goads, I picture a guy in sandals kicking those dried seedpods and having very bloody toes. That is how I looked after all those years, except that I had a bloody face and arms and hands. I had not stopped at kicking. I had wrestled with the intent of the prophecy.

I wrote this book in hopes that you will not have to do the same thing. I wrote this book in hopes that it will help you process your personal prophecies with a little less bloodshed. So if you are having difficulty understanding unfulfilled prophecies in your life—*read on*!

PROPHECY IN PERSPECTIVE:

The Voice of God

In the 1970s, many of us who had no previous experience with anything traditionally Pentecostal were introduced to the Holy Spirit and His gifts through the charismatic renewal. For my wife and me, this introduction came when we attended an interdenominational prayer meeting. We experienced a dynamic and beautiful move of the Spirit in the midst of worship that would change the course of our lives. One of the exciting parts of the monthly meetings was when the leader would ask what churches we all attended. It was wonderful to see how many different denominational groups were represented in what God was doing. It also meant that there were a lot of us involved in this move of God who had little to no formal training in the gifts of the Spirit.

Within weeks of being introduced to such things, we began to experience prophecy. Then through the 1980s and 1990s we, along with many others, learned the distinction between the gift of prophecy and the gift of the prophet. Recently, I found myself in a class for a couple of days with people from many different churches. At the conclusion of the class, the instructor casually asked the 25 of us how many had received prophetic words for our lives. Every person raised his or her hand. We have come a long way in the last 30 years.

As this phenomenon has unfolded over the intervening years, there have been many books written to help us walk through this experience. There are 22 books on the topic of prophecy on my bookshelf as I write this. I remember the excitement over some of the first material I got that simply gave me good working definitions of the various gifts and enabled me to understand the things that I was experiencing. One of the last books on this subject that I read was a college-level work dealing with serious biblical issues. Interspersed between the introductory booklets and the in-depth textbook are numerous books dealing with such things as methods, styles, protocol, and so on. Each is a good tool for helping the reader to understand different types of prophetic words, for dealing with the proper way to deliver prophecy, or for explaining the distinction and function of the gift of a prophet. All of them approach the subject from the point of view of the one delivering a prophecy or walking in the office of a prophet.

I have also attended nearly a dozen conferences over the years dealing with the subject of prophecy. It has been a blessing to hear firsthand some of the pioneers in the new age of the prophetic. What I learned at these events was supplemented by the encouragement and impartation you only seem to receive in person.

I have been blessed to be personally mentored by some men who are now recognized as both apostles and prophets. The things they have spoken directly into my life are invaluable, and I will always appreciate their love and input.

Finally, I recently received my master of ministry diploma from a Christian leadership institute. They do not have majors for their degrees but issue certificates of proficiency for specific areas of emphasis in selected study. I have a certificate of proficiency in prophecy hanging on my wall next to my diploma, which means I took a number of classes in the area of prophecy from several of the most recognized prophetic people in the Body of Christ.

This is not just a recitation of my life experience in the area of prophecy. There is a more specific reason why I have mentioned all of this. That is, in the wonderful exposure to teaching, training, and mentoring in the prophetic, all of it was directed toward how to receive and deliver prophecy more accurately and appropriately. None of my training was specifically dedicated to the issues of interpreting, judging, and implementing prophecy in a person's life. None of it was directed toward the issues from that point of view. That is not a criticism, it is just a fact. The books, courses, and conferences were not intended to address the issues from the point of view of the one who has received a prophecy. That is exactly what makes this book different. This book discusses prophecy solely from the perspective of the recipient.

To be fair, many of the books, conferences, and classes did touch briefly on how to respond to words given to you. My home church is also overseen by an apostle/prophet who often provides us with daily prayer guides that are designed to cover from 7 to 30 days, typically. They are always focused on how we can implement what God has been speaking to us prophetically. They are quite helpful. Still, from my experience, the proportion of material that addresses the subject of prophecy specifically from the point of view of the recipient is very small.

CONSCIOUS AND CONTINUOUS EFFORT

I believe this is one weakness that exists in the prophetic movement. We have had much less practical teaching directed at equipping people for rightly handling the prophetic words they receive. When we first began to experience the prophetic movement, many of us believed that if God said it and we kept moving forward, surely it would happen. Experience has taught us that it is much more involved than that. I read a commencement address given by C.S. Lewis once, in which he talked to the graduates about how life was like a very swift stream. He pointed out that you would not naturally make progress in moving upstream simply by entering the water. In fact, everything about the river would work to push you downstream if you just went with the flow. He pointed out that it takes conscious and continuous effort to advance in the stream of life. I try to live by this concept.

Likewise, I believe this approach could be appropriately applied to the implementation of prophecy in our lives. Most of us have learned that prophecies do not just happen because they have been spoken. The recipient has responsibilities in seeing the word come to fruitfulness. Yet as we have pointed out, there has not been a lot of material on exactly what those responsibilities are and how to walk out the process of implementation.

In the class I mentioned earlier, the instructor questioned how many of the people had prophecies that remained unfulfilled. Three-quarters of the people raised their hands. The process for working out and warring for your word is just as complicated as properly delivering a prophetic word. As important as delivering a prophetic word correctly is, if the recipient does not know how to see that word brought to fulfillment, the benefit is extremely limited. Especially in relation to personal prophecy, the ultimate goal is not to simply have a number of people properly trained to deliver wonderful prophetic words. While that is a good thing, the ultimate goal is to have every person who receives a prophetic word trained to judge the word and apprehend every blessing God intended through the word. For prophecy to be effective both the persons delivering the word and those receiving it must be trained for the specific responsibilities inherent in each of these positions.

There are two things we must learn to do when we receive a prophetic word:

1. We must judge whether the prophecy is a word from God (1 Cor. 14:29).

2. Once we have determined that it is a word from God, we are then admonished that we need to war for our word (1 Tim. 1:18).

The goal in writing this book is to create an instruction manual for doing these two things. We will learn how to correctly handle the word of truth (2 Tim. 2:15). We will learn how to contend until we apprehend, to travail until we prevail.

This book is intended to help us better discern, interpret, and implement prophecy.

Before we begin to address some of the specifics of how to do these things, we need to clarify some issues and definitions. We begin with two very important verses as we start our discussion:

1. *"He who belongs to God hears what God says. The reason you do not hear is that you do not belong to God"* (John 8:47 NIV).

2. *"My sheep listen to my voice; I know them, and they follow me"* (John 10:27 NIV).

These verses make it clear that every believer hears God's voice! Although I have met numerous Christians in the course of 30 years of ministry who emphatically complain, "I can't hear from God!" they were mostly mistaken. They were hearing from God; they just didn't recognize His voice and therefore never attempted to interpret or apply it. If you are one of those people, this book is for you.

Once, when we were in the process of making some changes in our ministry, we attended another local church for a season. There was one couple who attended our citywide regular Friday night ministry, and I was very concerned about them. They had only recently decided to follow Jesus and had just been baptized two weeks previously. I spent a good deal of time praying, because I feared they would be confused when I tried to explain what we were doing and why. We began attending the Sunday service at this other church, but I didn't tell them. On the morning of the second Sunday we were at this new church, this couple got up out of bed and flipped on the radio to the local Christian station. As it began to play, the man suddenly declared, "We are going to church this morning, and we are supposed to go to that church around the corner." When they arrived, they began looking through the parking lot to see if they recognized anyone's car. It didn't take them long to spot our motorcycles (several in our ministry rode motorcycles, including my wife and I). They were excited to realize that we were there. I had worried and prayed, and God had spoken. Problem solved. Now this man, being newly saved, didn't know he had heard the voice of God, but he had! So do you.

Each believer hearing the voice of God is the bigger picture, and prophecy is only a part of it. It is an important part, but only a part. Although this book is dedicated to understanding how to apply the prophetic and examining that process, we must step back and remember to view it within the larger panorama of hearing the voice of God.

HIS WORD, HIS WILL, AND HIS WAY

If we look at even a broader picture, we understand that what we need to learn most is how to be obedient. There are three parts to knowing what God is saying to us so that we can follow Him in obedience. There is His Word (the Scriptures). There is His will. David prayed earnestly about knowing God's will. "Teach me to do Your will," he pleaded with God in Psalm 143:10. Finally there is His way, which both David and Moses asked to have shown to them (Ps. 86:11, Exod. 33:13).

I once heard a man share about his work in Africa. He preached the Word of God to us: "Go ye therefore...." Although he preached the Word with the passion that only someone who has been there could, he could not preach what God's will was for every person in the room. There are many ways to be obedient to Matthew 28:19. God may want you to go to Africa, or He may just want you to go to the grocery store. He may want you to pray for missions, or He may want you to pay for missions.

After you have figured out His will for you in obeying Matthew 28, there are still myriad ways you could pursue your obedience. How are you supposed to get to Africa? Which clerk at the grocery store is the one God wants you to speak to? Are you supposed to form a prayer group for missions, or just add this particular ministry to your personal prayer list? Are you to give a one-time offering or regular monthly financial support? How much are you to give? Each person listening to this speaker that morning needed to hear the voice of God to determine His will and His way for implementing obedience to the speaker's preaching of the Word.

PREACH THE WORD

It is also important to understand the difference between His Word, His will, and His way, for the sake of our daily relationships. I once was part of a church where schooling of the numerous children was a hot issue. As in most churches, there were those who sent their children to public school and let the state worry about their education. Then there were those who home-schooled. Finally, there was a group of parents who were very involved through volunteering at their children's public schools. The opinions on the merits of each of these responses ran very high, until it occasionally spilled over into disputes regarding involvement in church-sponsored youth programs. I believe it would be fair to say that there were some judgments made by each group against the others. The problem? They did not understand that you can "preach" the Word but not the will or the way.

It is right and correct to preach that parents ought to take responsibility for their children. Most of us could go to the Bible and find references that make that position clear. But I have never seen a scripture that said, "Thou shalt home-school," or "Thou shalt volunteer." Each family needs to hear from God as to His will for them in working out their obedience. Even though they felt passionately about how they had been directed to act out responsibility for their children, they did not have the right to "preach" the will to other families and insist that they implement obedience in exactly the same way that God had required of them. Many disagreements in church life would be eliminated if people would learn the difference between the Word, the will, and the way, and only preach the Word, allowing every believer to hear God's voice and work out the will and the way that He has for them to demonstrate obedience.

THREE WAYS GOD SPEAKS

I have discovered that I need three terms to describe how God speaks to me regarding His Word, His will, and His way in my life. God speaks through His Word, through His voice, and through words of prophecy that God gives others on our behalf.

The Word

Based on Paul's usage, as well as other references, I use the term *the Word* to describe Scripture—the Bible. I love the Word. I have spent most of my adult life studying it. I believe it is the standard by which every other experience must be judged. It is the spring from which the will and the way of God flow. Everyone who seriously calls himself a believer must study and know what the Word says. However, it does not provide enough for us to know how to live out our obedience, apart from the voice of God.

The Voice

I recently read where someone said that we should not relate to the Bible as if it were the fourth person of the Trinity. Immediately, a common experience in my life came to mind. I travel a fair amount and, except when I am overseas, I try to call home every day. I still haven't figured it out yet, but my wife's life goes on while I am away. She still has to go to the grocery store and run errands, and many people invite her to dinner in my absence. So, occasionally when I call, I get the answering machine. I have to admit I hate listening to some stupid recording of my voice when what I need is to talk to my wife. I don't need a machine; I need my sweetheart! I need relationship, not information about how much I care about my own call and if I'd just leave a number...blah blah blah.

I believe it is that way with the Bible. The information is vital, but sometimes I need communication. I need to talk. I need relationship. I need the voice. Some one will object that you can hear the voice while reading the Word. Absolutely! That is what makes the Bible so unique. I can also hear the voice when I pray, or when I meditate, or when I stand in the high mountains of Colorado where I once lived, or when I sit in a crowded restaurant. We need to see that the voice of God is separate from the Word. The fact that I hear the voice of God when I read the Word does not make the Bible the fourth person of the trinity, any more than the fact that I hear His voice in the mountains makes him a tree; or the fact that I hear

His voice in a fast food restaurant makes Him a hamburger. As His sheep, we need to hear the Shepherd's voice in order to figure out His will and His way for us to be obedient to His Word, so the second term I use is *His voice.*

The Word of Prophecy

There is a third way that we can hear from God. The Bible teaches that others will sometimes hear the voice of God for us. This should never eliminate our desire to hear Him for ourselves, any more than the fact that there are teachers eliminates our need for personal Bible study. However, there are gifts given to us in the church to help us in our efforts to discern His will and way for us to be obedient. These are the gifts of the prophet, the word of knowledge, the word of wisdom, and the word of prophecy. These four gifts are another avenue for us to hear the voice of God. Therefore, I use the term *the word of prophecy* to refer to this method of hearing from God.

To summarize, there are three terms in my vocabulary. The Word refers to Scripture. The voice is when you hear from God for yourself. The word of prophecy is when someone else hears from God for you and shares it with you.

HARBOR LIGHTS

Let me conclude this chapter by giving you some tools for determining the will and the way in your life. Many years ago,

I heard a friend give a teaching on harbor lights. He talked about how, when you are out at sea and trying to get back into harbor, the lighted buoys are essential. They keep you from running aground on a hidden sand bar and spending hours waiting for the next high tide to lift you off. Note that I used the plural of the word *buoy* here. One of them will do you no good at all. You are always a part of the process in trying to determine direction for your own life, so one other confirmation alone will not be adequate in helping you determine how you are to go about being obedient. If you don't understand that, lay a couple of coins on the table right now.

One of those coins is you and the other is some fixed buoy of guidance. If you drew an imaginary line between those two, you would have a direction. The problem is, if you move the coin that represents you, while the buoy coin remains fixed, you could draw many different lines of direction. "Hello sand bar, here I come!" Now, put a third coin out there that is also a fixed buoy. Suddenly there is only one place you can put your coin so that the three of them make a straight line. You now have a safe direction. You need more than one point of reference, beside yourself, to safely navigate life.

My father-in-law was a commercial fisherman and I spent a fair amount of time fishing the pacific coast of northern California with him. I don't remember ever running into any harbor that had an entrance straight enough that just two buoys could mark it safely. In fact, in order to enter our homeport at

Bodega Bay, you had to cross a reef that extended from a head of land; once safely across that you turned 180 degrees to go up beside a jetty; at the end of the jetty, you made a 90 degree right turn and followed a series of buoys that led you in a long, hook-shaped path safely to the dock where we sold the fish. There was a whole series of buoys that made that passage safe. My experience is that this more accurately represents life than a simple two-buoy harbor. I've been stuck in the mud, both literally and figuratively, more than once (never with my father-in-law). I've learned that I want as many guidance buoys as I can get as I attempt to navigate through the treacherous waters of life on my way to the safe harbors He has for me.

I've come up with a list of guidance buoys that can help you find safe passage through life. This list of eight could have been combined to make six buoys or stretched out to make ten. This is just the way it turned out when I was sitting down to put this together. It is not presented in order of importance, nor is it intended to be an exhaustive discussion of any of these topics. It does assume that you are operating inside the parameters of the Word. I present these as helpful tools in determining safe buoys that will guide you into God's will for your life and His way for you to fulfill it:

1. *The voice:* This whole chapter is about the voice and the necessity of your hearing it (Rom. 8:16).

2. *The desire:* I don't believe that God generally goes around forcing us to do things that make us miserable. If our hearts are tuned to His heart, we will want to do His will. Desire cannot be considered an absolutely safe buoy by itself, but is often an indicator of timing (Ps. 37:4; 40:8).

3. *The prophet:* It is wonderful to receive a prophetic word from a proven, trusted prophet (more later in the book).

4. *The gifts:* The word of knowledge, the word of wisdom, and the gift of prophecy can all be useful in determining God's will and His way in our journey. Once again, there will be more on this later in the book.

5. *Pastoral counsel:* If you have never read all the Scriptures about counsel listed at the end of this paragraph, stop, get your Bible, and read them right now. You need a circle of trusted friends that you go to regularly for counsel. You should know who those

people are before you are in a crisis. This protects you from your own tendency to go to people who are most apt to tell you what you want to hear. They should be people who know you, know your weaknesses, and love you enough to tell you the truth. Your pastor should be one of these people. If you are married, your spouse should be another of these people. Get advice, proportional to the seriousness of the decision you are making. I once pastored a man who called me every morning to see if he should go to work that day (I put a stop to that before the week was out). Don't be silly, but don't be foolish, either, by not asking often enough. By all means, be sure to ask for counsel whenever you don't want to because that is a sure sign you need it. See Proverbs 11:14; 12:15; 15:22; 19:20; 20:18; and 24:6.

6 *The fruit of the Spirit:* Peace and joy are two powerful indicators. There is a beautiful picture presented in Isaiah 55:12: "For you will go out with joy, and be led forth

with peace…". This ties in with desire. It's fun to go out in the will and the way of the Lord. Remember that wisdom from above is first of all pure and peaceable. See Psalm 34:14 and Philippians 4:7.

7. *Confirmation:* Nothing is established by one of anything. We already discussed that when talking about the importance of relying on the harbor lights. Get as many of these buoys lined up as you can before approaching that sand bar (2 Cor. 13:1).

8. *Unity:* Where others are involved, there must be unity. This is especially true where a spouse is involved. I'm tired of hit-and-miss blessings in my life. I want *commanded blessings,* and they only come where there is unity. See Psalm 133.

You do not have to have every one of these in place before you navigating through life, but you should have the basics of the voice, desire, counsel, and unity in place. I definitely believe that we need to develop the attitude that the more harbor lights we have in place, the safer we are.

PROPHECY IN PERSPECTIVE

We have set the stage for examining prophecy more closely. We have put it in the perspective of every believer's need to hear the voice of God personally. Now, we can focus on the specifics of the gifts of the prophetic more closely without any fear of getting out of balance as we move toward a better understanding of what our responses should be to the words we have received.

CHAPTER ONE

1. Have you received prophetic words about your life that have not come to pass yet?

2. How has elapsed time and confusion about your prophecies interfered with your pursuit of them with conscious and continuous effort?

3. Taking a Scripture, such as Hebrews 10:25a, "not forsaking the assembling of ourselves together" (NKJV), and discuss the difference between preaching His Word, His will, and His way.

4. Can you add to the list of the eight buoys other things that might serve as harbor lights as you negotiate difficult waters in your life?

5. How does the awareness of these buoys put prophecy in perspective?

CHAPTER TWO

A PROPHETIC PARADIGM:

The S.O.A.P. Report

According to the dictionary, the word *paradigm* means an example or pattern. In common usage, it refers to the set we have established in our minds over the years of what would be the normal pattern of things. For instance, without thinking about it, we expect a ball to fall to the ground when dropped. If someone were to let go of a ball and it stayed in the air or rose, everything in us would shout a warning because this would be contrary to our paradigm.

I am told that we think via impulses that are called *synapses* in our brains that connect the words that make up our vocabulary. Words that are familiar to us have many connections to other words. These connections form the net that is our paradigm. When we are confronted by new words, ideas, or situations, we must form new connections. In the process, we are altering or expanding our paradigm.

Although our paradigms generally serve us so that we can move through life without analyzing every little detail, they can also limit us. One of the most prominent examples of a spiritual paradigm that needs altering is with the word *father*. Many of us, through bad experiences, have attached meanings with the word *father* that are not consistent with our heavenly Father's love, compassion, hope, and pleasure in us. In order to come into a full relationship with a compassionate, caring God, we have to deal with our old familiar connections to that word and to build a new paradigm through which we would relate to our heavenly Father.

BUILDING A NEW PARADIGM

I believe it would be most helpful for us to make the conscious effort to build a paradigm through which we naturally and comfortably relate to prophecy. I am going to suggest a model

I think is workable. This model will serve as a format for the rest of this book.

My wife has owned a medical transcription service for many years. Whenever you go to the doctor, there must be a hard copy report made of that visit. Most doctors dictate these reports into some kind of recording device and people like my wife listen and turn that dictation into a printed document. The thing that seems amazing is that the doctors remember what happened in every visit they have during a day, often doing their dictation at the end of the day. When you are in the doctor's office, it might seem like he or she is not even paying all that much attention to what is going on. Only once in my life have I seen a doctor take notes during the visit, and it was sort of distracting.

The way they remember all of the information without seeming to pay attention is that they have a fixed paradigm in their head that they use to make their reports. That helps them sort and store everything that comes at them during patients' visits. Because they have developed a paradigm, it has become almost automatic. God's prophetic people should be that well prepared to handle prophecy.

STRIKING SIMILARITIES

Actually, the similarities between a doctor visit and receiving a prophetic word are amazingly similar. The doctor you see may be someone you know well or may be a stranger you have never seen before. The doctor's style might vary from being very personal to being clinical and distant. Doctors may be attentive or seem absorbed in what they are doing. Whatever their bedside manner is, there will be an analysis of your situation made and a plan set in motion that could affect the rest of your life.

When you consider it, this is very similar to what you may experience when you receive a prophecy. The person sharing the prophecy with you may be your best friend or someone you have never met before. Almost every person I know who moves in a strong prophetic gift has a different style. Some are very personable and others seem like they are absorbed in listening to heaven as they deliver the word they are hearing. Personally, I enjoy the diversity of styles. Regardless of these factors, there must be an analysis made of the whole experience and a plan must be formed for how to integrate it into your life. The only difference between a doctor's visit and receiving a prophecy is that the analysis and plan are much more your responsibility with the latter than with the former. So you need a clear paradigm for evaluating and implementing prophecy.

THE S.O.A.P. REPORT

The paradigm/report that a doctor uses on a general office visit is called a *S.O.A.P. report*. That is an acronym for *subjective, objective, assessment,* and *plan.* Let's look at this format and see how we can adapt it to build a paradigm for prophecy.

The Subjective

The first thing a doctor will ask you is why you are there. Doctors want to know what you are experiencing subjectively. You explain where you are hurting or the difficulty you are having. It is not your responsibility to be scientific or analytical. You are just sharing what you have experienced. This is the *subjective* part of the visit that will provide the information that will become the subjective part of the report.

With every prophecy there is a subjective part of the experience. You may have feelings about the manner in which the prophecy was delivered. You may experience a sense of the presence of God. What is spoken may touch you deeply or not. You may have an emotional reaction to the words spoken. Although all of these are perfectly legitimate experiences, they are subjective experiences. The fact that they are the subjective part of the experience in no way diminishes their importance. I have received words when I felt the presence of God so strongly that even though I did not fully understand the content of the prophecy, I meditated on them for years until they became clear. Without the strength of this subjective experience, I might have not been so diligent and might not have eventually come to an understanding of what God was saying to me. Considering the important role these subjective aspects may play, they need to be evaluated.

The Objective

The *objective* portion of a doctor's report covers all the findings made during the examination. It includes your vital signs, observations the doctor made while looking into your eyes and ears, and consideration of the sound of your lungs and heart. It differs from the subjective because it is not determined by how you feel but by what the thermometer and stethoscope objectively tell the doctor about your symptoms. The report is systematic in that it usually starts at the top with your head and works its way down your face, neck, torso, and ends up with your lower extremities, depending on the extent of the examination. This systematic approach allows the doctor to once again do this almost automatically.

The objective part of a prophecy is also not about how you felt about the experience. It is about what actually happened and the words that were spoken. Did the prophecy include any prophetic acts? Did the experience include things like the laying on of hands? But most importantly, what were the actual words used? We will discuss in greater detail later in the book how you go about making a record of the objective part of a prophecy. Suffice it to say now that it is usually the most important part of the prophetic experience, and as such, we need clear guidelines as to how to handle the experience and information if we are going to be able to get the most from the experience.

The Assessment

After the doctor has heard your subjective complaints and gathered as much objective information as the doctor feels is needed about your symptoms, he or she is then prepared to make an assessment or diagnosis about your condition. The goal of the *assessment* is usually a simple, straightforward definition, but in difficult cases the doctor may only be willing to make a tentative diagnosis and order more tests to clarify or confirm what the initial exam indicates.

There are a couple of interesting factors in the assessment portion of a doctor's report. The assessment section is usually typed in all capital letters. This is intended to draw attention to it as the most important part of the report. The second characteristic is that whereas the subjective and objective may be quite lengthy and involved, the assessment is often one word or phrase. These two characteristics emphasize that we are at the heart of the issue. The assessment is intended to be clear, concise, and emphatic. Sometimes such a clear diagnosis is simply not possible and the doctor is forced to speculate and comment on possibilities. Although that may be necessary in certain situations, it is always the goal to try to be as specific and concise as possible.

What part of receiving a prophetic word corresponds to the assessment in a medical report? I believe it corresponds to what the Bible calls judging the word in First Corinthians 14:29. Every word must be judged. Once again, we will go into more detail later in the book. For now let us emphasize that if we have learned how to collect and sort all the information from our prophecy both subjectively and objectively, the job of making a concise assessment or judgment of the prophecy will be much easier. Our goal, too, should be to make as concise a judgment as possible. It is not always possible to do this with a prophecy either, so we may be forced to make a tentative evaluation and wait for more information (revelation) to be added in the future. We must keep in mind that the goal is to make as clear a judgment as the current revelation allows us. The clearer we are able to be in making our judgment, the easier it will be to move on to the next section.

The Plan

The final section of the medical report is the plan. What is the doctor going to do about your condition? Is it a viral syndrome for which he or she will explain symptomatic measures that will give you some relief while the illness runs its course? Will the doctor prescribe medications? Will he or she order more studies or recommend surgery? No matter how skilled your doctor is, the plan can only be as effective as the assessment that was derived from the subjective and objective portions of the exam. Furthermore, the effectiveness of the plan is usually conditional on you doing your part in implementing the treatment.

The same is true with a prophecy. Once you have considered your subjective feelings about the experience, analyzed the objective words spoken to you, and made a judgment regarding the prophecy, you need a plan to see that you receive all the benefits God intends for you from the word. As we stated earlier, the assessment is the most important part of a report to the doctor, but to us as patients, we need a plan! We just want to know what to do to get well. The same is true with prophecy—we need a plan. If you do not develop a plan, there will be little benefit from the first three parts of the analysis. At the same time, your ability to make a good plan is dependent on how effectively you have performed the first three elements in our prophetic paradigm. Here is where most prophetic experiences break down. Few of us have been well trained to develop a plan of action regarding prophecies, and like the medical treatment plan, the success of our apprehending everything God has for us through a prophecy depends on how well we implement the plan.

We are going to look carefully at all four of these steps and help you build a paradigm that will aid you in interpreting and judging prophetic words so that you can develop a plan for implementing them and hopefully gain everything that God intends for you through them. In the next chapter, we will begin to look at the subjective elements of prophecy in detail.

CHAPTER TWO

—–⫴–—

1. Define what a paradigm is.

2. Give an example of how paradigms are usually good.

3. Describe how each of the following terms applies to a visit with your doctor and then the parallel it has with prophecy:

    a. Subjective

    b. Objective

    c. Assessment

    d. Plan

THE SUBJECTIVE, PART ONE:

An Environment for Prophecy

In the previous chapter we defined the subjective part of receiving a prophecy as how the experience affects you. There are at least three elements that make up the subjective part of the experience. The first is how the actual spoken words may impact you. They may cause anything from a deep emotional response to puzzlement. We will discuss these responses later in the book.

Second, you may sense the manifest presence of God as the prophecy is delivered to you. This may come as anything from an overwhelming physical experience to just the sense that He is there speaking to you in the gentlest way. We must not mistake the strength of these kinds of experiences with the significance of the prophecy. It may be that the simplest prophecy evokes a deep emotional response, while a deeply penetrating word just creates a sobering sense of His presence. I remember years ago, watching a visitor at church all through a rather dynamic worship service and powerful teaching. Nothing seemed to be breaking through this person's exterior shields. Then during a final song at the end of the service someone rose and prophesied a simple, "God loves you." As I watched, the person began to weep. She gave her life to the Lord that evening. Remember, by definition, prophecy is not primarily about the experience but is about the words God is speaking to you. We must resist the temptation to score a prophecy by how many goosebumps it raises.

The third aspect that impacts us subjectively is the whole atmosphere that surrounds the experience. Different things may affect that atmosphere. What other things are going on in the room, the demeanor of the one delivering the prophecy and your attitude are all things that may affect your perception of the environment when the prophecy is delivered. Usually, it is more affected by the one giving the prophecy than the other issues. This is probably the least considered aspect of prophecy, but I believe it is very important for us to understand the environment God intends to be surrounding the whole experience of receiving prophecy. The focus of this chapter is on the environment in which prophecy best flourishes and brings forth the most fruit.

Before we begin talking about the best environment for prophecy, we need to make one issue very clear. Receiving a personal prophecy is *your* experience. You are center stage. God is talking to you. Since that is true, how you feel about the experience is of utmost importance. So you need to remember that you are in charge of the experience. In the end, you get to sort through the experience and decide what it means to you.

The most basic sphere of government that God has established is *self-government*, called self-discipline or self-control in the Bible. Whenever anyone deals with you, they are entering the sphere of your self-government and need to honor your authority there. This knowledge should give you freedom to receive a prophecy without fear. You are the one who will judge the final experience, so approach it in relaxed confidence.

Since it is our goal to present a guide to discerning, interpreting, and applying prophecy, let's look at the proper environment for prophecy. Unless we understand the basic atmosphere in which prophecy is supposed to thrive, we can never hope to accomplish one of the first tasks we must do, which is analyzing the subjective portion of every prophecy. We must understand the subjective portion of our experience in receiving the prophecy before we are concerned with making any judgment regarding it's content.

MIXED MESSAGES

The problem is that there have been so many mixed messages from both prophetic people and other leaders about the prophetic realm. Some prophetic people have looked to Elijah's demeanor on Mount Carmel as a model of how they should deliver prophecies. They seem to forget that he was dealing with false prophets of a false god. I do not think this is a very good model for working with people you are supposed to be encouraging.

One of the first "prophetic" people I ever met was a man who had changed his name and adopted a first name, a middle name, and another middle name of Old Testament prophets. He always spoke in a very deep voice that resonated out of his chest as though coming through a hollow pipe. One time while he was at a service station, some people pulled in, rolled down their window, and said to him, "We're lost…." Without waiting for them to finish, he spoke in that deep voice and said, "I know," followed by a litany of King James English exhortations for them to be saved. The people just rolled up their window and drove off. This man may have given goosebumps to me as a new believer, but he was not using a very effective model of prophecy.

I also spent a lot of money once to fly halfway across the country to attend a prophetic conference for a week. All but one of the international church leaders who spoke at the conference spent that whole week telling those of us who were prophetic what a nuisance we were on our best days and how dangerous we were on our worst. I did not learn how to better administer my gift. I just walked away feeling more isolated and unsure. Isolation and rejection are not good planks to use to build a platform for ministry.

Somehow I knew that both of those extremes were wrong and have spent years trying to discover the best atmosphere in which prophecy could help mature the saints. Like most passionate prophetic people, I have battled my own Mount Carmel tendencies, which have wanted to flare up and burn anything I saw as false or unjust. With the help of many, I have also waged warfare against the rejection and accompanying hurts, so that I would not minister out of them, either. If neither the priest nor the offering were to have any scab on them in order for the offering to be acceptable to God, how much more do we need to be sure that we are not ministering out of any of our own hurts? Refer to Leviticus chapters 21 and 22 for a discussion of regulations concerning priests and acceptable offerings.

THE ENVIRONMENT OF PROPHECY

What is the environment in which prophecy will flourish in our lives? What is the atmosphere in which the prophetic will produce the most fruit in the lives of people? We have eliminated anger, judgment, isolation, rejection, and hurts. But what is the biblical model?

We must begin by looking at a verse from First Corinthians 14:3, "But everyone who prophesies speaks to men for their strengthening, encouragement and comfort" (NIV). Strengthening, encouraging, and comforting—those are the stated purposes of every ministry through the gift of prophecy. Those are the words that are used to describe the environment where most prophecy must occur. We recognize that those who walk in the office of a prophet may on occasion minister correction and direction, but even this should be done with the same goal of strengthening, encouraging, and comforting. Where these are present, prophecy will help people grow and mature.

UNDERSTANDING GOD'S ATTITUDE

I believe that one of our major problems is that we do not understand how God feels about us. His attitude is clearly stated in John 3:16,17:

For God so loved the world that He gave His only begotten Son, that whoever believes in Him should not perish, but have eternal life. For God did not send the Son into the world to judge the world, but that the world should be saved through Him.

Here His attitude is stated very clearly. God loves us! He loves us so much that He sent His Son so we would not perish but could *live!* The message of verse 17 is not quite as clear. The Greek word *judge* in the phrase "not…to judge the world" could be translated as "decide." With that understanding we could read the entire phrase as "not to make a decision about you and me yet." Therefore we could interpret (not translate, but interpret) the second half of this verse to mean that God sent Jesus so that all possibilities would still be open to you in Him. We are so prone to make negative judgments about others, life in general, and ourselves, but God's attitude is not one of judgment but one of love and hope for the possibilities for our future.

One of my favorite scriptures has become Jeremiah 29:11: "'For I know the plans I have for you,' declares the Lord, 'plans to prosper you and not to harm you, plans to give you hope and a future'" (NIV). If God is for us, who can be against us? If God loves us so much He has made plans for our future, why would we allow anyone else to rain on our parade? In fact, why do we rain on our own parade so often? God has not given up on you yet. As a matter of fact, He is still holding all options open for you. Your future is wide open. I hope you feel the joy these statements are intended to bring. I hope you never go back to making judgments about others or to letting them make judgments about you. This is God's heart: Because of His great love for you, your future is still wide open in Jesus! Let's read John 3:16 and 17 one more time from *The Message* before we move on:

> *This is how much God loved the world: He gave his Son, his one and only Son. And this is why: so that no one need be destroyed; by believing in him, anyone can have a whole and lasting life. God didn't go to all the trouble of sending his Son merely to point an accusing finger, telling the world how bad it was. He came to help, to put the world right again.*

Do you see an environment? Do you perceive an atmosphere? Do you sense an attitude? Can we answer the question, "What is the environment of prophecy?" Yes we can! It is an environment of love, hope, and faith that all your possibilities are still open to you in Jesus. That is the environment in which prophecy and its fruit will flourish. That is where we will discover His plan and future for our lives. That is where prophecy will be most effective in helping us mature.

FIRST CORINTHIANS 13

Now I understand why the chapter 13 of First Corinthians is in between chapters 12 and 14. I used to wonder how this "love chapter" had gotten placed between two "gift chapters." Could it be that it belongs right there in the middle because love is supposed to be at the heart of all the gifts?

I did something the other day just out of curiosity that I want to share with you. I read First Corinthians 13:4-7 in my Bible and inserted the word *prophecy* in the place of the word *love*. It fit and helped me understand things more clearly than I ever had before. *Prophecy* is patient, *prophecy* is kind, and is not jealous; *prophecy* does not brag and is not arrogant, *prophecy* does not act unbecomingly; *prophecy* does not seek its own, *prophecy* is not provoked, *prophecy* does not take into account a wrong suffered, *prophecy* does not rejoice in unrighteousness, but rejoices with the truth; *prophecy* bears all things, believes all things, hopes all things, endures all things.

Wow! That is an atmosphere where prophecy can flourish and cause us to grow into maturity. I think we have discovered the environment for prophecy. Any prophecy that is not born, grounded, and rooted in love is a false prophecy!

NOT AN EXCUSE

This does not mean that there will never be a word of correction. This does not mean that there will never be a word outside of your comfort zone. This does not mean that there will never be a word that challenges you to change your life or your outlook. On the one hand, I want to make it clear that you never need to receive ministry coming from a bad attitude or woundedness. You need to recognize it and respond accordingly. On the other hand, I do not want to give you an excuse to reject words just because they may have some unpleasantness to them. Correction can be love. A challenge can be love. An expectation for change can be love. Kicking you out of your comfort zone may be the most loving thing anyone ever did for you. So look for love in every prophetic utterance, but do not look for excuses to reject any of them.

IN SUMMARY

We started this chapter with the goal to discover the environment or atmosphere in which prophecy could flourish and bear the most fruit in people's lives. We know now that the environment in which prophecy must exist and flourishes is the same as God's love for us and His hope for our future. I hope the information in this chapter will help you see clearly the atmosphere in which prophecy should be given. This should give you the information you will need to evaluate the subjective part of your prophetic experiences. You should be equipped to sort through this subjective part of the experience and decide which parts to keep and which parts to discard.

Do not expect or demand that everyone deliver every prophecy perfectly. After all, we are just human vessels trying to deliver the message of God to one another.

This should free you to respond to the more important subjective elements of the experience. Does the prophecy touch you emotionally? Do you feel the manifest presence of God? Do you experience an inner agreement with the prophecy? Remember, these are important parts of the experience but they are still subjective. It is best to make an analysis about these portions of the experience as soon as possible. Time has a way of causing them to lose their sharp edge and blur them. You want to remember exactly how the experience affected you subjectively, so make some notes even before you begin to examine the objective parts of the prophecy. It will help you both when it comes time to make an overall assessment of the prophecy and to develop a plan.

CHAPTER THREE

1. Name the three elements that make up the subjective part of prophecy.

2. Why is it dangerous to grade a prophecy by how many goosebumps it raises?

3. Who is in charge of the experience of you receiving a prophecy?

4. What are the three words used in First Corinthians 14:3 that describe the environment in which prophecy will flourish?

THE SUBJECTIVE, PART TWO:

Prophetic Accountability

I n the last chapter we talked about the subjective environment or atmosphere that surrounds the delivery of a prophecy. We looked at the issues from the demeanor of the one delivering the prophecy to your own mood or attitude. We now want to look at some issues regarding the *person* who may be prophesying to you. This may not be a purely subjective issue but it probably fits in this part of our S.O.A.P. grid better than it does anywhere else.

MEASLES OR MUMPS?

A simple illustration will prepare you for what we are going to discuss in this chapter. One of my mentors used to warn us that if a person had the measles, it was irrelevant if they preached the mumps, because you would still catch the measles from them. The message in that little saying is that impartation goes beyond the words spoken. I believe that any deeply intimate experience involves impartation. Receiving prophecy can be a deeply intimate experience so that there can be impartation. Remember, we said in the last chapter that you are in control of the experience of receiving a prophecy. Just as you are able to control the intimacy level of a conversation with a stranger at the grocery store, you can control the intimacy level of the experience of receiving a prophecy.

The question is, "What should you be on the lookout for?" This chapter will help answer that question. I will begin by giving you two extremes of bad prophetic protocol and then move to the positive description.

PARKING LOT PROPHETS

The first time I heard someone use the term *parking lot prophet*, I did not know whether to laugh or cry. I used to live in a place where the spirit of independence was strong. There were self-proclaimed prophets who were not members of any church but would go around to different churches drawing people aside to prophesy over them. Therefore, I instantly knew that this term did not refer to improper *locations* for receiving prophecy but to improper *attitudes* of some who want to deliver prophetic words. To me, the term refers to someone who does not want to acknowledge or operate within normal spheres of church government. They want to chase you down in the parking lot after church to "give you a word," where they or the prophecies they give are less apt to have to be subject to proper accountability. I am not suggesting that prophecies given by respectful, accountable persons are suspect if they are given in a parking lot. In fact, I wish that all believers were prophesying everywhere, in parking lots, in grocery stores and in their neighborhoods. I am only suggesting that you avoid prophecies given by people with the kind of attitude just described, no matter what location you happen to be in.

THE MAN OF GOD

I once attended a meeting where a "front man" preceded the well-known international speaker to the stage to inform us that "the man of God" was there that night. He added that he alone was anointed to minister and that all ministry or prayer between attendees was forbidden even after the meeting was dismissed and we were departing. For years I have heard well-known speakers declare that the day of the superstar is over. Now we have to start acting like it.

I do not believe that in ordinary circumstances, either the *parking lot prophet* or the *only man of God* attitudes represent the appropriate prophetic protocol. A true prophet promotes having his or her prophecies judged and wants to see every believer become proficient in prophecy.

A CERTAIN CENTURION

We must begin in understanding proper prophetic protocol by asking, "Where does your authority come from?" By definition, the *act of prophesying* is speaking for God. Where do you get the authority to speak for God? That is not a rhetorical question. It is one that must be understood and answered.

A story in Matthew chapter 8 presents a very important principle. An officer of the Roman army, with the responsibility for 100 men, had a servant who was terribly ill. He approached Jesus to request a healing, a bold move that reveals this man's understanding. Jesus agreed to come right over to his home and heal the servant. The centurion said he was not worthy to have Jesus enter his home. More importantly, he understood that it was not necessary for Jesus to come to his house.

His next statement reveals the depth of his understanding:

For I also am a man under authority, with soldiers under me; and I say to this one, 'Go!' and he goes, and to another, "Come!" and he comes, and to my slave, "Do this!" and he does it. Now when Jesus heard this, He marveled, and said to those who were following, "Truly I say to you, I have not found such great faith with anyone in Israel" (Matthew 8:9-10).

This officer understood that just as his authority came from Rome and went all the way back to Rome, so Jesus' authority came from God and went all the way back to God. He understood delegated authority. He understood that delegated authority flowed to him from Rome and through him to his soldiers. He understood that Caesar did not have to show up personally to reinforce every command he gave to the soldiers under him. He understood having authority because you are under authority. He understood that this universal truth applied to Jesus as much as it did him. Jesus acknowledged this understanding of the flow of authority as "great faith."

THREE KEYS OF PROPHETIC PROTOCOL

One time as a child, while playing in the hills, I drank from a beautiful bubbling stream, only to round the next corner and discover a dead deer lying in the stream. I worried for days that

I would get sick or perhaps even die. Talking to my friend did not lessen my fears. He used it as an opportunity to torment me. I did not consult with any adult, fearing how stupid I would look. Fortunately, since you are reading this book, you already know I did not die. I am glad to also inform you that I did not even get sick.

You are probably wondering what this disgusting story has to do with prophecy. I did not tell you this story to upset you. I told it to you as a warning! Before you drink from any-one's prophetic stream, you had better know what is upstream—that means knowing from where his or her authority flows. With whom are they connected? To whom are they accountable? If they are offended by such questions, there is a certain Roman officer they need to learn something from. Furthermore, if they are offended at such questions, I would wait to get a drink from someone else's prophetic stream. Parking lot prophets may not be as harmless as they seem. They may even have measles.

Authentic prophets should follow three key areas of protocol:

1. They are under a higher church authority.

2. They respect spheres of authority

3. They do not violate privacy issues.

Let's look at each of these in more detail.

Being Under Authority

The first and most important issue in prophetic protocol is being under authority. Every authentic prophetic ministry needs to have accountability to some form of authority. It may vary from situation to situation, but the principle is made clear in First Corinthians 12:28, "And God has appointed in the church, first apostles, second prophets, third teachers, then miracles, then gifts of healings, helps, administrations, *various* kinds of tongues." Notice the word right in front of "prophets" in this verse. It is *second*. If prophets are second, then that means someone else must be first. It is important to also notice that in this list it is not God who is first but some other person. Every parking lot prophet will insist he or she is submitted to God, but that is not the issue. Every prophetic ministry in a local congregation must be submitted to the local leadership, and if someone claims to be a prophet, that person must be accountable to some form of apostolic government. Remember—check upstream before you get a drink. You do not even want to risk getting sick.

Respecting Spheres of Authority

If prophetic people operate in the first issue of prophetic protocol, the second is easy. Once again, we need to say that prophetic ministry must always respect the sphere of authority where it is operating. We mentioned this issue in the last chapter, but it is so important that it is good to mention it in here also. As we said before, it is not the purpose of this book to go into the details of the issue of spheres of government. If you are being ministered to prophetically, those doing the ministry must respect the sphere of your individual self-government. When a child is being ministered to, the parental responsibility in the sphere of family government must be yielded to also. Those who operate under authority themselves usually understand these concepts.

Privacy

The third issue that should govern prophetic protocol is privacy. There are some things that just should not be spoken publicly. There is always some corner or some small room available after the meeting where deeply personal ministry can and should take place. Remember, prophecy is for encouragement and strengthening, not shaming and embarrassing.

WHAT SHOULD I DO?

Fortunately, most of us have experienced ministry that was sensitive, respectful, and encouraged personal responsibility in judging, interpreting, and implementing prophecy within appropriate spheres. Unfortunately, some of us have been the recipients of ministry that was condescending and that challenged you if you dared to question the authenticity of the word. Some of you may be recalling those incidents with discomfort. I hope I have helped you understand that your dis comfort was appropriate. Perhaps you find yourself still asking, "What should I have done?" I want to be careful here, but at the same time I want to empower you to govern the sphere of your own life. I see three different levels of ways you can avoid ministry that you are not comfortable receiving:

1. I have just gotten up and walked out of meetings where I felt the ministry was inconsiderate of those being ministered, too. Yes, it was embarrassing, but when you consider the seriousness, it was worth the momentary discomfort.

2. I have also been in meetings when walking out was simply not an option. In those situations, you need to understand that every sphere of authority has the ability to simply close the gates around itself. Usually when you do that, others sense it and will not try to push through.

3. If they are not sensitive to this, you always have the option of saying, "I am

not comfortable receiving ministry right now." Wasn't there a national ad campaign that preached "just say no"? Personally, when I am ministering randomly to a group of people I don't know, I always ask the person for permission before I give a word. It is just polite and considerate. In the final analysis, that sums prophetic protocol up completely.

As we conclude this section on the subjective part of receiving a prophecy, remember—you are in charge. You are responsible to evaluate the environment and accountability of anyone you allow to impart something into your life. You do not need to fear these things. You are now equipped to judge the subjective part of the experience, keeping the good and discarding what is not.

CHAPTER FOUR

~~\|/~~

1. What is the point of the illustration of measles and mumps?

2. What is the point of the author's disgusting story of drinking out of a stream as a young boy, only to later discover a dead animal upstream from where he had taken the drink?

3. These two stories combine to place emphasis on what three prophetic protocols?

4. Do you have the option of declining ministry if you do not feel comfortable that the minister is operating within these three protocols? How might you accomplish that?

5. How would you "close the gates" around yourself if you did not want to receive ministry?

THE OBJECTIVE, PART ONE:

Analyzing Prophecy

We need to be trained to correctly analyze prophecy. "Do your best to present yourself to God as one...who correctly handles the word of truth" (2 Tim. 2:15 NIV). I realize that in this verse Paul is talking to Timothy about correctly handling Scripture, but if, as Peter says, Scripture is "a more sure word of prophecy"

(2 Peter 1:19 KJV), how much more should we be accurately analyzing our other words of prophecy that we receive?

A RECORD OF THE WORDS

Now that we have moved into the objective portion of analyzing your prophecies, we are not concerned with the atmosphere or your feelings but with the actual words spoken. I have used the phrase *actual words spoken* because, in my experience, my memory of what was spoken has proved to be quite different than the actual words spoken. I know that because most of the important prophecies that have been given to me are on tape, and every time I listen to one I am surprised by how poor my memory is of the content of the prophecy.

Taping is certainly the preferred method of recording the "actual words." Sometimes a tape recording is just not available. If that is the case, you should try to write down, immediately after the prophecy is given, as accurate an account of the actual words that were spoken as you can. It is useful to get help in doing this from family or friends who may have heard the prophecy. Remember, memory is poor at best, especially after a few years.

SCREENING TOOLS

Now that you have as accurate an account as possible of the words used, we need some simple screening tools like the doctor's thermometer or stethoscope to help us objectively evaluate the content. I would like to present you with five different parameters that you may use to help you analyze prophecy. Someone will surely object and accuse me of trying to put God in a box. Let me assure you, I have no interest in building a box for God. For that matter, I have no interest in a god who would fit in any box I could build. What I am trying to do is give you some grids to help you analyze virtually any prophetic word in order to help you understand it. Most prophecies can be measured against all five of these parameters. If you do this, you will be well on your way to understanding the prophecy and how to handle it with wisdom.

There is one last thought we need to consider before we look at these grids. So far we are just putting tools in your toolbox. It is very tempting to want to jump right into judging, interpreting, and applying prophecy. Equipping you to do those things is the purpose of this book, but I want you to be equipped with all the right tools before we ever start that job. I used to do finish carpentry on multi-million-dollar homes, and believe me, having the proper tools available and sharp before you start a job is critical to the quality and beauty of the finished job. So be patient.

THE PARAMETER OF PROPHECY OR PROPHET

The first thing you must look at deals with an issue we mentioned earlier. The question you must ask is, "Was the prophecy delivered by a Christian using the gift of prophecy or by a recognized prophet?" We stated earlier that the domain of the gift of prophecy was generally limited to strengthening, encouragement, and comfort. We used First Corinthians 14:3 as our text for this. "But everyone who prophesies speaks to men for their strengthening, encouragement and comfort" (NIV). We said that prophecy given by someone recognized as walking in the office of a prophet may also contain direction and correction. A prophet may also prophesy encouragement.

This first parameter helps you divide a prophecy into two major groups for further analysis. It also allows you to consider if a well-meaning believer may have gone beyond their gifting in trying to deal with issues that are not in the domain of the gift of prophecy. This determination is critical to judging the word.

We will now move through four parameters moving from the simplest form of encouragement to more complex prophecies.

THE PARAMETER OF ENCOURAGEMENT AND INSPIRATION

As previously stated, every true prophetic word will be spoken in love to strengthen, encourage, and comfort. We already dealt with this in our discussion of the environment where prophecy flourishes, but we need to apply it now to the words spoken. Did the content of the words encourage, strengthen, and comfort you? If this parameter is not firmly established in your understanding, go back and read Chapter 3 again until it is clear to you. Remember, you cannot reject a prophecy just because it stretches your comfort zone, but if you determine it is not founded in love and is not helpful for your encouragement and strengthening, you are well on your way to knowing how to respond to it. (We will discuss in a future chapter how to handle an unwelcome prophetic word.)

The vast majority of words are going to fall into the category of encouragement and inspiration. They are going to have the goal of strengthening and comforting you. Whenever I have asked an audience I was teaching how many of them could simply use more encouragement in their lives, almost every hand went up. Although this is the most common type of prophecy, we do not want to devalue it in any way. These audiences' responses indicate how much we need it in our lives.

Let me give you two examples of encouraging inspirational prophecy. I once was praying for a young man in our congregation who worked for the railroad. I received a mind's eye view of a train. I asked God what that meant and felt the response, "Tell him he is on track and on schedule."

A couple of weeks later, this same young man and I had an opportunity to minister together to another individual. He "saw" an archer with his arrow nocked and at full draw. I was asking the Lord for an interpretation when I realized that in archery terminology, the shooting of an arrow is called a *release* and that once you have pulled a bow to full draw, it is very difficult to hold it there for very long. So I interpreted the meaning of this picture to be that there was a release coming soon for the gentleman to whom we were ministering.

Both of these words were simply meant to be inspirational and encouraging. There have been many times in my life when I would have loved to know that I was on track, on schedule, and that a release was coming soon. Have there ever been times in your life when such a word would have been like a cool drink of water in the desert?

THE PARAMETER OF DIAGNOSIS/PROGNOSIS/PLAN

Returning to our use of medical terminology, I find the three-part parameter of *diagnosis, prognosis,* and *treatment* to be very helpful. With this screening tool, we can see the working together of the different prophetic giftings for a complete solution for an individual. We are moving out of the area of the gift of prophecy and into that reserved for the prophets. The line between these two is not always distinct because part of this parameter may be seen as encouragement, but the last part is clearly moving into the area of direction. I personally believe the line between the domains of prophecy and the prophet is not as distinct as we presented earlier. However, we needed to define it clearly so you would be able to recognize when someone has overstepped their gifting. When nearing this distinction, you just need to pay attention! Remember, you are being equipped to do that.

Diagnosis

Diagnosis often comes in the form of a word of knowledge. The simplest example would be if the Lord revealed that an illness was caused by bitterness. This could be a part of almost any prayer for healing.

I also remember a much more involved situation when a young husband invited my wife and me over to pray for a long-standing problem in his life. On the way to his home, I felt impressed by the Lord that this young man needed a dramatic demonstration and therefore I was not to let him say anything by way of explanation when I arrived. After a brief greeting, I told him this and we sat and started praying and waiting on the Lord.

Over the course of the next hour, I received three visions of incidents that had happened in this young man's life. The first was startlingly detailed and graphic. The other two were less detailed, but were still specific. They were all about important encounters between this young man and people important in the development of his life—a spiritual leader, a parent, and a group of peers. The enemy had used these encounters to plant a time bomb in his mind. At an inopportune time, it would have been used to blow up his and his family's lives. As I began describing in vivid detail the first scene, he was astounded because he had never told anyone about this incident. When I completed that story, he went from shock to sobbing tears. As I relayed each of the other two, he shook his head in awe and confirmed the incidents had occurred just as the Lord had shown me.

As powerful as this experience was for him, it was *just* diagnosis. It clearly demonstrated that God knew what the problem was but did nothing to present a solution. So we proceeded to prognosis.

Prognosis

Prognosis is a statement of what the future holds (i.e., what are the chances of recovery?). It is not enough to tell people they are sick. We do not need spiritual gifts to know that. What we need to stir our faith is a statement of hope for our recovery.

Prognosis will often take the form of prophecy. Returning to our previous example of an illness being tied to bitterness, I find that after sharing the connection between an illness and its root, and getting the person's agreement, I often have an assurance from the Lord in my heart that if the person repents, he or she will be healed. I am able to offer the person this encouragement, and usually the person is eager to cooperate through repentance. We have seen many healed using this model.

In the illustration involving the young husband that I received three visions for, my wife and I were led to begin prophesying over this man. We prophesied extensively about his future in exactly the area of the former attacks. The Lord spoke of His marvelous plans for this young husband, his wife, and his family. The prognosis for his recovery was extremely good! Although this might seem like all that was needed, we were still not done.

Treatment Plan

We often stop without considering the need for a treatment plan. Although a word of knowledge may give us a detailed picture of what is wrong, and prophecy may let us know what God's plan is, we need the word of wisdom to know how to get from where we are to where we need to be. We need a treatment plan. Here the gift of the word of wisdom should be encouraged and cultivated. It may be the most underdeveloped and underused gift there is.

Returning once again to our illustration involving a connection between an illness and a root, this step may be the most involved. Is the Lord showing you that if the person repents right now, He will heal right now? Is the problem just between God and the person you are praying for, or are there other individuals involved? Is there reconciliation that must be pursued before you will be released to pray for the person's healing? Perhaps, if the person repents before God and you pray for them, that person will be instantly healed but will still need to pursue reconciliation with others.

How are you supposed to know what to do? The word of wisdom will give you a treatment plan that will complete the whole picture.

In the situation involving the young husband, we did some binding and loosing with this young man. After praying, we gave some instructions specific to the area of attack. He was prepared with the full compliment of gifts to move forward with his life. You should run your prophecies through this grid to distinguish these three aspects of this type of prophecy.

THE PARAMETER OF CATEGORIES

There are three different types of categories a prophecy might fall into. The first one relates to timing. There are "now" and "future" prophecies. The other two categories have to do with whether or not a prophecy addresses an issue you have already considered. They are the categories of a confirming prophecy or a new prophecy.

Now or Future

When you receive a prophecy, one of the most important things you must decide is whether it is a *now prophecy* or a *future prophecy.* This applies to prophecies that have moved beyond simply being encouraging. This screening tool alone will determine much of how you respond to and apply a prophecy.

Unfortunately, timing can be one of the most difficult issues to deal with in prophecy. Remember, for two thousand years the Spirit has been saying in the hearts of believers that Jesus is coming back "soon." On a more personal level, a review of the prophecies in Abraham's life leads you on a 125-year journey. So it really is a very personal issue when evaluating any category that deals with timing.

If it is a *now* prophecy, it is intended to impact your life in the immediate circumstances and provide an agenda for current action. A *future* prophecy may require you to "hide it in you heart" for years. This does not infer that future prophecies do not require current responses.

A prophecy may refer to both your past and your future and still be a now word. Think about this example: "From your mother's womb I have been preparing you to be a teacher, but for you to go where I have planned, you must know My word." If you received such a prophecy, how would you measure it against this parameter? It refers to your past, but it also certainly points to the future. Interestingly, you could categorize it as a now prophecy. I would receive it as an exhortation to get to know the word—that is, the Word, who is Jesus—through relational prayer and study of the Bible. This prophecy may refer to the future but it gives a present agenda for making the future possibilities a reality.

It would also be appropriate to look at this example as being a future prophecy. Future prophecies can be a tremendous help when you have to battle circumstances. Do not let circumstances overpower the future prophecies you have received. Overpower the circumstances with the future prophecies. When discouragement or disappointment comes into your life, get out those future prophecies and be encouraged to press on. Recite them to the heavens. They are mighty weapons against such attacks.

Also recognize, as we alluded to already, that your future prophecy often depends on some present action on your part. I have a real concern that many people may think that categorizing something as a future prophecy means that there is nothing they need to do now. Not so! Every word at this level requires some immediate response.

Just as we said that God might speak a current prophecy by referring to your past or the future, He may also speak a future prophecy in the present tense. God speaks of things that are not as though they are (Rom. 4:17). A good example of this is found in Judges 6:12. "When the angel of the Lord appeared to Gideon, he said, 'The Lord is with you, mighty warrior'" (NIV). Let me remind you that when the angel of the Lord spoke to this "mighty warrior," he was hiding in a wine vat as he worked and required repeated changes to fleeces to overcome his uncertainty. He did go on to become a mighty warrior before the Lord was finished with him. The point is, God saw him that way and spoke it in the present tense, even though it could easily be seen as a future word.

Many times I have witnessed God begin to raise up humble leaders and listened to their response be this: "I just do not see myself that way." That is because they probably were not up to the challenge of what God was speaking to them at that moment. God was speaking about the future as if it were already present.

It is not always easy to distinguish between now and future prophecies. Do not worry, because the real question is always, "What should I do now to respond to this prophecy?" Finally, do not hesitate to ask for that word of wisdom in determining the timing for any prophecy and the immediate response you should make to it.

Confirming Prophecies

Many times we need a little encouragement to just keep going, so God will send us confirming prophecies. We get tired and need a fresh touch. Although confirming prophecies are wonderful, we should not become dependent on them. If you have received clear words in the past about a particular subject that has not yet come to pass, do not think there is necessarily something wrong with you if God has not mentioned it lately. Receiving repetitive confirming prophecies should not be seen as a sign of approval or maturity.

Universally, parents sit on the floor talking silly to their toddlers and trying to get them to take a few steps, but I have never seen the parents of teenagers doing the same thing. In fact, they usually seem to be trying to get their teenagers to stand still long enough to get in a few words with them! Maybe you have not had a confirming word in awhile because God is expecting some maturity out of you.

Let me give you a personal example. For years I feared I was the guy that everyone resented at meetings. I was the first person to get picked to receive prophetic ministry before the speaker ever got started. Then there were times when the speaker would talk to me all through the sermon, too. At the end of the meeting, I sometimes got one more prophecy. Everyone wanted to confirm my prophetic calling. I got to where I was so embarrassed by it, I would sneak into meetings late and sit in the back and pray that God would say something to my friends. Looking back, I needed that much confirmation. I was a mess and had an awful lot of hard schooling to go through before I could even approach what God had planned for me.

Then I went through a ten-year period of silence where no one ever gave me a confirming prophecy. I wondered if I had done something wrong. I wondered if I had missed it. Although there were some dark days in those ten years, I just kept plodding on. Then, when I had the outline of this book, an initial title, and the first chapter written, a guest prophet came to our church and prophesied over me. He spoke a confirming word once again about my life and calling. He proceeded to say that I had a book in me and actually spoke the temporary title I had chosen on this book.

Why after ten years? Well, I needed encouragement to keep writing this book. My Father understood that I was insecure about starting to write a book. How loving our Father is! So enjoy words of confirmation when they come, but do not panic if they stop. Grow up! Keep being obedient! Mature!

Before we move to the next section we need to provide a segue. Some have taught that prophecy can only be confirming. They teach that God cannot say anything new to you through prophecy. This simply cannot be taught textually. It ignores one of the primary functions of prophecy in Scripture. I believe that it is taught sometimes in an attempt to reinforce your self-government, but I believe we have made a solid presentation for your self-government without stripping prophecy of an important function.

New Prophecies

So let's consider when a brand new idea comes to you through a prophecy. What if someone speaks to you something you have never thought of before? We were just talking about the joy of all those confirming prophecies. You know what? The very first time those ideas were presented to you, they may have been new!

Allow me to make some suggestions about dealing with a new idea presented to you in prophecy. *Do not* reject the idea categorically because you never thought of it before. *Do not* sell your house and move to Afghanistan on the basis of one new prophecy. *Do not* hold the idea too loosely. *Do not* hold it too tightly. *Do* apply careful discernment. *Do* go back and review the harbor lights of Chapter 1. *Do* hide the word in your heart and see what happens. *Do* be patient.

If God presents a brand new idea to you through a prophecy, He will begin to unfold the plan and open doors for you. There will be confirmation that comes either through more prophecy, through other harbor lights, through open doors, or through your own heart. You may have just received the first indication of an exciting adventure. Hang on and enjoy.

THE PARAMETER OF REVELATION

Now we are moving into an area where we need to exercise more caution. These prophecies require more careful attention. Let's divide this screening tool into three subcategories. These are prophecies that contain words of correction, words of direction, or words for protection. We will look at these one at a time.

Correction

First, we will consider the area of correction. As mentioned before, prophecies containing correction are not normally in the arena of the gift of prophecy but of the office of a prophet. These words can be simple or quite complex. I once received a word of knowledge that an individual was involved in an adulterous affair. I give this example here only to help you understand prophecies that contain correction. There are many other examples we might use.

Recently I was discussing a tense situation with a friend I receive as a prophet. During this conversation, I said something rather tersely. My friend looked at me and said, "What is that?" Because I respect this individual, I had to spend some time examining what had come out of me. It led to revelation of some issues that went far back into my life, and I am pleased to say I got some deliverance through this situation. My friend would probably not say that he gave me a prophetic word of correction, but I chose to relate to it that way and received a blessing by doing so. We should not fear correction, but rejoice in the resultant liberty (Heb. 12:11).

When dealing with any kind of overt correction, the situation demands great sensitivity and strict adherence to rigorous standards of protocol. We must also remember that even these types of prophecies must be delivered with full realization that the one receiving the words has the right and obligation to judge them.

Direction

The second category under prophecies containing revelation is direction. These prophecies will almost always come through someone in the office of a prophet. There is never a word of direction that would be considered insignificant.

Recently, a woman from our congregation came to me following a service and asked if I could pray for her about involvement in a particular para-church ministry. As we waited on the Lord together, I realized what a unique combination of personality, motivational gifts, and ministry gifts this woman had. It was obvious she could be very effective in the ministry she was considering. Even as simple as this was, I took her to our pastor before sharing this with her and told her to consult with her husband before making any decision. Things such as finances, job changes, or geographical moves would fall into this category as well. Also, issues involving marriage, children, and future fivefold ministries would be part of this category.

Protection

The Lord will sometimes give us prophecies that are really just signs that say, "WARNING!" He wants us prepared for what is about to occur in our life. He is acting like any good father would. He wants to protect His children. It is my opinion that this category of prophecy is usually personal enough that it would normally come through either someone close to you or someone operating in the gift of a prophet.

A good example of this type of prophecy comes from Acts 21, when the prophet Agabus prophesied to Paul. Agabus told Paul that when he went to Jerusalem he would be bound and, by inference, imprisoned. God wanted Paul to know what was in store for him. Understandably, Paul's friends believed this was a word of protection to warn him not to go to Jerusalem. Paul discerned that this was not the case, but was simply a warning to prepare him emotionally and spiritually for what was ahead. Prophecies that fall into the category of protection could be given either to get us to change our actions or to just prepare for the future. In either case, our Father is just protecting us.

They may also be given to us so that through prayer we can avert the impending danger. I once received a dream that was quite vivid and clearly a warning of an attack against my ministry. I rallied intercessors and am happy to report that we never saw the manifestation of this attack materialize. The goodness of God had warned us of this impending attack, but we were able to outwit the enemy through intercession.

Any prophecy involving a warning must adhere to our description of the atmosphere of prophecy that we presented earlier in this book. Doom-and-gloom prophecies that do not encourage us with hope are not from God. It is just that simple.

THE TOOLS

I think your toolbox is about half full. Now remember, these are just tools. As I mentioned earlier when I was a carpenter, I loved my tools. I loved getting new ones. I almost did not want to use them. I wanted to build a fancy oak box with lined drawers, carry them to jobs, and show them off. I knew that with use they would get dull and scratched. Some beautiful, intricate woodwork was created, though, and that was the goal, after all.

We need to put these new spiritual tools to work. You should use them when they are appropriate for the job. Never forget that it is your life that you are working on. You are His workmanship. Your being perfected into His image is the goal. Prophecy is not the end. It is just a help along the journey. Do not get distracted by tool worship. So let's add a few more tools in the next chapter before we go to work.

CHAPTER FIVE

1. How does applying the parameter of prophecy versus prophet help protect us from a well-meaning believer who has gone beyond his or her gifting?

2. The vast majority of prophecies will fall into the parameter of _____ and _____.

3. Define the three parts of the third parameter that are based on medical terminology—diagnosis, prognosis, and treatment plan.

4. The parameter of categories is important because _____ can be one of the most difficult issues to deal with in prophecy.

5. Why is it particularly important for us to note when a prophecy falls within the parameter of revelation?

THE OBJECTIVE, PART TWO:

Three Basic Principles, Three Common Questions

As we conclude our objective examination of the actual words spoken in our prophecies, we must have a clear understanding of several issues. Our responses to prophecies must reflect sound biblical understanding. I have often seen situations or been asked questions that reflect that we do not yet have these issues clearly settled in our minds.

So in this chapter we will discuss three basic principles of prophecy and three often-asked questions. You should understand these so that they are reflected in your future analysis of prophecy. We need to make these simple truths part of us so that they become a natural response. If you remember these three principles and the answers to the three questions, they will give you secure guidelines in relating to prophecy.

All Prophecy Must be Judged

There are two words in this heading that are absolutes: *all* and *must*. This principle applies to *every single* prophecy that you will ever hear. It does not matter who gives it. It does not matter what "signs accompany" the prophecy. It simply does not matter. *All* prophecy *must* be judged. It does not matter if your all-time favorite Bible teacher, or your pastor, or the most accepted prophet you know or even an angel prophesies—*all* prophecy *must* be judged. "And let two or three prophets speak, and let the others pass judgment" (1 Cor. 14:29).

Let's address how this affects those giving prophecy. One of the conditions those who prophesy automatically agree to is that other people are going to have to pass judgment on what they say. If they do not like those terms, they should not prophesy! In other words, prophecy must be given open-handedly in a submitted attitude and in a manner that encourages that it be judged. If you encounter someone who has any attitude different than the one described here, be very cautious about receiving prophecy from such an individual.

I have heard people introduce what they were about to share by stating that they were instructed "not to submit their word to any man." That person either "heard" wrong or was hearing from someone besides God. Every word must be submitted so that it may be judged. You should view any word prefaced with this kind of statement very suspiciously, if you do not reject it categorically. (There is the slight possibility that the one delivering the word is an immature novice and has just attempted to overcome their nervousness with this kind of statement, in which case they need specific instruction.)

The second aspect of the principle that all prophecy must be judged is directed toward you as the recipient of prophecy. We have often used the illustration when training people to prophesy that they are supposed to be good mail deliverers. They should be absolutely responsible to make sure that the message is delivered as sent. However, once they deliver it, they are not responsible for what you do with your mail. Your postal carrier does not come by your house to make sure you paid the bills he delivered. Once he delivers them, they become your responsibility. It is the same with prophecy. We want careful delivery, but once that is completed, responsibility goes to the one who received the prophecy. You are responsible to judge any prophecy you receive personally.

That does not mean you cannot seek help or input. In fact, you need to get counsel and input in the process of judging and applying any word of serious consequence. We discussed this in detail in Chapter 1 under the heading of Harbor Lights. It simply means that once you receive a prophecy, you have accepted responsibility for that word both to judge it and apply it.

ALL PROPHECY IS IN PART

"For we know in part, and we prophesy in part" (1 Cor. 13:9). Gaining a clear understanding of this second principle of prophecy would save many people a lot of confusion and misapplication. This verse sounds pretty simple when you read it, but what does it mean practically? It means that a prophecy never gives us the whole picture. It does not cover every aspect of the topic. It means that any prophecy is only partial.

Have you ever heard the story of the four blind men who ran into an elephant? They were puzzled as to what they had encountered, having never "seen" an elephant before. Each began to describe what their hands told them about this new creature. One was holding his tail and described it as a small broom-like thing. Another argued, as he put his arms around one of the elephant's legs, that this animal was a tree. The third man was puzzled by the first two descriptions as he ran his hands over the expanse of the elephant's side and expressed that this animal was like touching the side of a barn. The fourth man, having gotten a hold of the elephant's trunk, insisted that the others were mistaken and that this creature was very similar to a snake.

They all were "seeing" in part. No one description was wrong, but neither was it complete. So it is with prophecy. We never see the whole picture, and even though our description of what we "see" may be completely accurate, it is never complete. You must factor this principle into the response that you make to prophecy. That sounds simple, but too often we want to make decisions on a word we receive without looking for those other parts. Consequently, we may reject it because it seems too narrow or we may overapply it beyond its proper scope.

Allow me to give you a common illustration. A married couple receives a prophecy that God wants to use them to minister to other marriages, but first He is going to work on their marriage. I have seen couples get this kind of word and react strongly against it with exclamations that they were humiliated by the accusation that there was something wrong with their marriage. Apply this principle—prophecy is in part. Is there any married couple who can claim that there is not some area where their relationship could use improvement? The prophecy was not a blanket accusation against their marriage.

It was in part. It was a statement that there was a "part" of their marriage to which God was going to bring improvement. My wife and I have been married for more than 40 years and we have a wonderful marriage, but I wish God would show up and say that He was going to be working with us to make it better.

Can you see how important it is to understand these principles and apply them to the prophecies you are receiving? That is why the first chapter in this book discusses the necessity of you hearing from God for yourself. That is why we mentioned that there are many ways to hear God, and prophecy is only one piece of the puzzle. We talked about the need to have more than one harbor light to navigate successfully. Prophecy is in part, and you are going to have to figure out which part a prophecy plays in your life as you attempt to apply it.

GOD OFTEN SPEAKS IN RIDDLES

This third principle of prophecy is a little confusing. So we will begin by giving you some biblical examples of what we are talking about in this principle.

In Numbers chapter 12, Miriam and Aaron began to speak against their brother, Moses. God dealt with this seed of rebellion quickly and called them to come to the tent of His presence. He spoke to Miriam and Aaron and told them that He normally speaks to His prophets in dreams, visions, and dark sayings, but He spoke to Moses face to face. He proceeded to challenge them as to how they would dare criticize Moses.

The importance of this story for us is that few of those, if any, who prophesy to us get to hear from God face to face like Moses did. They "hear" in dreams, visions, and dark sayings. In other words, there is often some obscurity in the way God talks to us when He gives us prophetic words.

An excellent illustration of this is found in Jeremiah 1:11-12, which says, "And the word of the Lord came to me saying, 'What do you see, Jeremiah?' And I said, 'I see a rod of an almond tree.' Then the Lord said to me, 'You have seen well, for I am watching over My word to perform it.'" Most of us would read this and ask what seeing an almond branch has to do with God's faithfulness to watch over His word. The answer is nothing—unless you speak Hebrew and know how to interpret dark, hidden sayings. In Hebrew, the spelling of the word *almond* and the word *watching* are only one letter different, and they are pronounced almost identically. God is using a pun!

Some of you are responding right now with a huge question in your mind. "Why would God do such a thing?" Let me offer you two possible answers to that question. First, it forces us to be dependent on a personal relationship with Him for interpretation. Remember that God's highest goal is for you to have personal relationship with Him. He does not want you to have a really great relationship with a prophet. He wants you to have relationship with Him! He does not want us to become prophecy junkies. He wants us to be addicted to relationship with Him. These kinds of prophetic words will drive you to Him for understanding and application.

Second, these kinds of hidden, riddle-type messages force us to turn to one another. Often, the person receiving such a revelation is not able to interpret it with the greatest accuracy. This forces us to be humble and open in submitting our revelations to others. I know that although I can interpret word pictures I receive for others, when I receive one for myself, I often struggle with the interpretation. This forces me, although my revelations are sometimes very personal, to go to friends and ask for help to understand the revelations. It can be a very humbling experience, but one that is good for our relationships. So in my life, God accomplishes two things by speaking in dark riddles: pursuit of relationship with Him and with my friends. Not a bad bonus on top of whatever encouragement I receive from the revelation itself.

Before we move on, let me just reemphasize that you need to remember to apply these three principles of prophecy. Receiving a prophetic word is supposed to be a fun, positive experience. It is supposed to encourage and build you up. It is not supposed to create confusion. If you approach each word with these principles, it will go a long way toward making your experience more pleasant and profitable.

THREE COMMON QUESTIONS

Now that we have established the framework, let us see if we can find answers to the three most common questions I have been asked over the years.

Can a Prophecy Be Wrong?

Of course it can be! Implied within our first principle that all prophecy must be judged is the understanding that there is the possibility that a prophecy may be wrong, or at least a portion of it may be. If there were no possibilities that they could be wrong, why would we be instructed to judge them? Consider the instructions given in First Thessalonians 5:19-21, which states, "Do not quench the Spirit; do not despise prophetic utterances. But examine everything *carefully*; hold fast to that which is good." If you examine something carefully and hold onto the good part, the inference is that you discarded the parts that were not so good. You judged the prophecy just like you were supposed to do. Remember, prophecy comes through imperfect people; hence there will be varying degrees of mixture in them. That is why Paul gave this instruction for us to sort through the prophecies we receive and keep what is good.

There is a very real possibility that part of the prophecy may be wrong, but the overall message would be correct. You may need to "hold fast to that which is good" and disregard the rest. There is a biblical example of exactly this process. We referred to these verses in the last chapter but need to see them in their entirety here:

"And as we were staying there for some days, a certain prophet named Agabus came down from Judea. And coming to us, he took Paul's belt and bound his own feet and hands, and said, 'This is what the Holy Spirit says: In this way the Jews at Jerusalem will bind the man who owns this belt and deliver him into the hands of the Gentiles.' And when we had heard this, we as well as the local residents *began* begging him not to go up to Jerusalem. Then Paul answered, 'What are you doing, weeping and breaking my heart? For I am ready not only to be bound, but even to die at Jerusalem for the name of the Lord Jesus.' And since he would not be persuaded, we fell silent, remarking, 'The will of the Lord be done!'" (Acts 21:10-14).

There are several things we want to notice in this account. The first is that there is a prophetic word given by Agabus, a man who is acknowledged as being a prophet. In this word/picture, Agabus says that Paul will be bound by the Jews if he goes to Jerusalem and turned over to the Gentiles. Paul's friends immediately interpret this word to mean that he should not go and with tears beg him to heed this warning. Paul, understanding prophecy, knows it is not up to his friends to interpret and apply this word but it is his responsibility. He does not deny the correctness of the overall word

but emphatically rejects the interpretation of his friends. He
judges it to be a warning to prepare for what is ahead and not
a directive to change his plans. He examines it carefully and
holds fast to that which is good.

Furthermore, if we follow this story to its conclusion, we
discover that part of the details of this prophecy seems to be
inaccurate. Later in the same chapter is the record of what happened when Paul arrived in Jerusalem.

> *And while they were seeking to kill him, a
> report came up to the commander of the
> **Roman** cohort that all Jerusalem was in confu-
> sion. And at once he took along **some** soldiers
> and centurions, and ran down to them; and
> when they saw the commander and the soldiers,
> they stopped beating Paul. Then the com-
> mander came up and took hold of him, and
> ordered him to be bound with two chains; and
> he began asking who he was and what he had
> done"* (Acts 21:30-33).

Agabus prophesied that the Jews would bind Paul and
turn him over to the Gentiles but what actually happened was
the Romans bound Paul and took him away from the Jews
before they killed him. The prophecy was generally correct
but some of the details were not. The prophecy was entirely

true in the figurative sense but not literally accurate in every detail. To whom did the responsibility fall to judge this prophecy? To Paul, the one who received it. This story serves as the perfect example of discerning, interpreting, and applying a prophecy.

Is Prophecy a Guarantee?

No, prophecy is not a guarantee. I have heard people say both jokingly and seriously, "I cannot die because I have unfulfilled prophecies." That statement reflects a lack of understanding. A prophecy is an expression of God's intention and the possibilities associated with them—not a guarantee. There are several reasons why a prophecy may not come to pass.

Perhaps the prophecy is a preventative word of warning. Jonah's resistance to going to Ninevah is a classic example of this type of situation. Jonah's complaint was that if he went and prophesied against Ninevah and they repented, he knew God would cancel the prophecy and then Jonah would look like a false prophet. In fact, that is exactly what happened.

We can see that there are times when it is good that a prophecy does not come to pass. As I mentioned earlier, I once had a prophetic dream of warning about an attack that could materialize in my life and how I should respond to it. I immediately notified my overseer, my ministry peers, and my personal intercessors. There was only one small incident that may have been related to this dream, but no serious manifestations.

Through prayer and faithfulness any further expression of that dream was canceled.

Furthermore, prophecy almost always requires response from you before it will come to pass. Many prophecies come in the "if/then format." Most of the promises of Scripture contain this kind of clause. We may not like to hear this, but if you do not perform the "if," then you do not receive the "then." Since you have taken responsibility for the prophecy once it was delivered, it may require direct or indirect obedience from you.

We will discuss later how a prophecy may require maturity in you before it can be fulfilled. There are many factors that may affect the outcome of any prophecy. You may, by your choices, receive only part or none of the fruit of a particular prophecy.

Furthermore, sin may prevent a word from coming to pass. Moses' life offers us an example of this type of interference. "Now the Lord said to Moses in Midian, 'Go back to Egypt, for all the men who were seeking your life are dead,'" Exod. 4:19. That is a direct, instructional word from God. So we can assume that God was going to bless Moses on his trip back to Egypt, right? Not necessarily! Look at verse 24 of the same chapter. "At a lodging place on the way, the Lord met Moses and was about to kill him," (NIV). Why would God try to kill Moses when he is on a trip that God told him to take? God was trying to kill Moses because he had sinned by not circumcising his son. Sin can interrupt the course of a prophecy coming to pass.

These three illustrations of why a prophetic word is not a guarantee should help you understand that you need to discern, interpret and apply the prophetic. Remember that confession is not the same as possession. Only obedience to the process will guarantee the results.

A Prophecy from Ten Years Ago Still Has Not Come to Pass—Why?

One of the most poignant passages of Scripture that I read from time to time to inspire my courage and patience is Joshua 14:6-14:

> *Then the sons of Judah drew near to Joshua in Gilgal, and Caleb the son of Jephunneh the Kenizzite said to him, 'You know the word which the Lord spoke to Moses the man of God concerning you and me in Kadesh-barnea. I was forty years old when Moses the servant of the Lord sent me from Kadesh-barnea to spy out the land, and I brought word back to him as it was in my heart. Nevertheless my brethren who went up with me made the heart of the people melt with fear; but I followed the Lord my God fully. So Moses swore on that day, saying, 'Surely the land on which your foot has trodden shall be an inheritance to you and to*

*your children forever, because you have fol-
lowed the Lord my God fully.' And now behold,
the Lord has let me live, just as He spoke, these
forty-five years, from the time that the Lord
spoke this word to Moses, when Israel walked
in the wilderness; and now behold, I am eighty-
five years old today. I am still as strong today
as I was in the day Moses sent me; as my
strength was then, so my strength is now, for
war and for going out and coming in. Now
then, give me this hill country about which the
Lord spoke on that day, for you heard on that
day that Anakim were there, with great fortified cities; perhaps the Lord will be with me,
and I shall drive them out as the Lord has spoken.' So Joshua blessed him, and gave Hebron
to Caleb the son of Jephunneh for an inheritance. Therefore, Hebron became the inheritance of Caleb the son of Jephunneh the
Kenizzite until this day, because he followed
the Lord God of Israel fully.*

Imagine this 85-year-old man standing in front of the
one friend who had stood with him in one of the most difficult
times of his life. There was history between Joshua and Caleb.
They had a bond of camaraderie born out of adversity. Caleb's

fervor for the word that had been given him did not diminish over a 45-year wait. At 85, he still had fire in his soul to lay hold of the promise of God. He was still ready to take on the giants in the land, if need be. What an inspiration!

Furthermore, consider that from the time Samuel first anointed David to be king, it was 24 years before he actually took the throne. Abraham's life is a 125-year saga of expanding and unfolding prophecy. In my own life, there was over a 30-year span between the first time someone spoke to me that there was a prophetic call on me and the time when other leaders ordained me as a prophet.

Unless a prophecy contains a specific date or time frame, do not disregard it just because more time has elapsed than you expected. You may need to evaluate your continuing response to a prophecy but do not throw is out because of the time that has passed. Some wise person said, "God measures growth, not time."

There may even be circumstances beyond your control that are not allowing a particular prophecy to come to pass. Remember in my case the Lord said that I would be hidden until both the church and I were ready for the message He had for me to deliver. It is possible that I might be ready before the church is. Be careful not to make excuses for yourself if there are changes you need to make before a particular prophecy can be fulfilled. Do not make excuses for yourself, but if I never see the fullness of some prophecies in my own lifetime, I will hold them until the end. I hope that with my last breath I will have Caleb's courage to proclaim that they will still come to pass in my future generations.

The terms used in prophecy in relation to time may infer something to us that are very different from what God means. For instance the word *suddenly* in Acts 2:2 might suggest to casual observer that the coming of the Holy Spirit was without forethought or planning. It might infer that it just happened spontaneously, when in reality it had been prophesied long before. The apostles had been in training for three and a half years. The 120 had been praying waiting and believing for weeks. They were right before God and right with one another. So they can be viewed as the right people, in right standing, in the right place, at the right time, and it "suddenly" happened.

What about the word *immediately* in Mark 4:29 used in relation to the harvest? Do not forget that the ground had been plowed and prepared; the seed planted; it had time to germinate, sprout a stalk, leaves, and finally a head; then it matured and ripened. Then it was "immediately" harvested.

Because of Saul's disobedience, he was told that "now" his kingdom would not continue (1 Sam. 13:1-14). That "now" turned into 38 years before David took his place. In fact, 24 years before David's ascension to the throne, Saul was told that the Lord was tearing the Kingdom of Israel from him "this day" (KJV).

As we can see, God's terminology differs greatly from ours. After all, we must remember that God speaks of things that are not as though they already existed (Rom. 4:17).

We must learn two things about allowing God's timing to unfold. First, our "faith" cannot force Him to work on our timetable. You can pray; you can confess; you can shout and praise, but His timetable is still His. In fact, the second thing we need to learn is that we do not want to "help things along" through strife. If we do, we will produce an "Ishmael" instead of the fruit of the promise (Gen. 16). The fruit of strife is always conflict and never peace. Remember, God may miss a lot of opportunities to be early, but He is never late.

CHAPTER SIX

1. What are the two most important words in the statement, "All prophecy must be judged"? Why?

2. How does the story of the four blind men who ran into an elephant illustrate the truth that all prophecy is in part?

3. Why does God speak in riddles?

4. Can a prophecy be wrong?

5. Is prophecy a guarantee?

THE ASSESSMENT:

Judging Prophecy

Now that you have gathered and analyzed information in the subjective and objective portions, you are prepared to make an assessment. If you have completed those first two parts of this process, this third and most critical part will be easy.

This chapter will present you with a list of questions. The final and most important question will be, "Do you believe the prophecy or any part of it was from God?" You will answer each question based on the information we have analyzed in the subjective and objection portions. These questions will incrementally answer that last question before you even get to it. The questions will be asked sequentially to correspond with the issues as we discussed them in the subjective and objective portions. Let's begin!

What Do You Discern Was the Spirit Behind the Prophecy?

Was it the Holy Spirit? Was it from the Father who believes in you and is rooting for you out of His vast love and hope for your future? How much mixture was there in the delivery? Was the spirit of the person delivering the prophecy also expressing love and faith toward you?

If you discern that it was not the Holy Spirit or was not coming from love and faith, do not receive the word into your spirit. If you discern there was some small amount of mixture in the delivery that was not based in love and faith, set that part aside and hold onto the part that is good. Remember, mature people can eat the fish and spit out the bones.

If you discern it was the Holy Spirit speaking out of the Father's love, then you have just received a precious gift.

The next few questions apply to both the subjective and objective portions as we have viewed them in the previous chapters. They apply to both the spirit in which the prophecy was given, as well as the content of the actual words spoken.

DID THE PROPHECY REPRESENT THE MORAL CHARACTER OF JESUS?

At first, this question appears to be only a slight variation of the previous one. Although you cannot separate the spirit of Jesus from His moral character, by rephrasing the question we can look at things from a little broader angle.

Is there anything in either the delivery or the content that is contrary to the character of Jesus? Does the prophecy in any way suggest a response from you that is inconsistent with the moral character of Jesus? Did the person delivering the prophecy do or say anything that was inconsistent with the character of Jesus?

Reframing the question to involve the character of Jesus makes it more serious to me. If there were any measurable mixture in the prophecy that was inconsistent with the moral character of Jesus, I would just let it go and not receive it. We do not want to overreact to the issue of mixture, but there are some things that can pollute the whole prophecy to the point that it is not worth the risk to try to retrieve any of it. A small drop of strychnine can be deadly even if it is part of a wonderfully beautiful piece of chocolate candy. Besides, if a message God is trying to speak to you gets polluted, He will say it again in a safer environment.

DOES THE PROPHECY RESPECT YOUR SPHERE OF SELF-GOVERNMENT?

Does the prophecy usurp your authority or will in any way? Does it attempt to overpower you in word, deed, or attitude? Is the prophecy or the delivery manipulative or controlling in any way? Does it show respect to the other spheres of government in your life, such as a spouse or local church?

Anyone who prophesies and any prophecy that is from God will be under authority and therefore will respect other spheres of authority, especially your sphere of self-government. If any person or prophecy tries to overpower you, do not receive it.

DOES THE PROPHECY ENCOURAGE OUTSIDE INPUT?

Does the prophecy and the delivery encourage you to seek confirmation from other harbor lights, as we mentioned in the first chapter? Does it encourage you to be responsible to judge it? Is it all done in openness and in the light?

If the prophecy or the delivery in any way suggests being

secretive about what is being said, there is something wrong. That is not walking in the light. Do not confuse what we are saying here with the need to respect privacy sometimes, but even prophecy that addresses private issues should encourage further outside input.

DOES THE PROPHECY COMFORT, ENCOURAGE, AND STRENGTHEN YOU?

If you have gone through the previous steps of analysis, you already know the answer to this question. It is included here again to remind you that even a prophecy that was bringing you correction will ultimately offer you these elements in the love and faith it expresses toward you. A word of correction that is from God will offer you hope. This leads us to the next question.

IF THE PROPHECY FALLS INTO THE CATEGORY OF A WARNING, DID IT OFFER YOU HOPE AND A PLAN OF ESCAPE?

Was it presented in such a way that there seemed like there is no way of escape? Did it offer you encouragement and hope? Did it strengthen you to be victorious?

If a word of warning is just doom and gloom, I would not receive it into my spirit. God, who still believes in you even when He is correcting or warning you, always offers hope for our future.

IS THE PROPHECY CONSISTENT WITH BIBLICAL TRUTH?

Does it in any way suggest a response from you that would violate biblical teaching? Does the content agree with biblical truth?

Remember, this must be true not only in content but also in attitude. If it is not consistent with biblical truth in any way, it is not from God. If you are unsure about the answer to this question, just ask someone you know who is well versed in biblical truth to go over it with you. In fact, that is good advice if you are at all unsure about any of the issues we have raised in these questions.

DO YOU BEAR WITNESS TO THE PROPHECY?

Before you answer this question, allow me to explain what the term *bear witness* really means. The term as it appears in the Bible comes from the Greek word *martureo*, which means to be a witness or to give testimony. Being a witness at a trial is not based on how you feel about a situation, but what you saw and experienced.

Likewise, in judging prophecy, bearing witness is not really about how you feel about the experience. It is not about measuring goosebumps. You have truly done much in regards to "bearing witness" as you have processed a word through the steps we have covered in the book. This does not mean that you fully understand every detail of the prophecy and how it will all work out. It means that you have been responsible to rightly handle the word that was given to you. After your thorough consideration and analysis of the things we have covered, you are truly prepared to give accurate testimony about the legitimacy of a prophecy. Therefore, you are prepared to answer this question and then the final question.

DO YOU BELIEVE THE PROPHECY OR ANY PART OF IT WAS FROM GOD?

Like the doctor doing a S.O.A.P. report, you ought to now be able to give a short, concise answer to that question in most situations. As we said earlier, there might be some situations where you have to put some of this away in your heart and wait for further information, but normally you will be able to answer this question in the simplest of terms. I hope you have been truly empowered to say with confidence, "Yes," to most of the prophecies you have received.

It is equally important that you feel empowered to reject any prophecy or portion of any prophecy that has not made it through this process. If you have prophecies that you need to reject, just do it mentally, in your heart/inner self, and in prayer. It is really important that you unplug your inner self from any words that were hurtful. You can do all this through prayer. You do not need to fear prophecy you reject. The only legitimate fear might be of not knowing how to judge prophecies, but you are now equipped to do that with confidence.

The only part left to discuss is how to develop a plan for the prophecies that go beyond simple encouragement and inspiration, pointing to things in your future. So the next chapter will begin to discuss the plan as we follow our S.O.A.P. report model.

CHAPTER SEVEN

1. Who is responsible for the final assessment or judging of a personal prophecy given to you?

2. How might a prophecy that demands a certain response from you violate your sphere of self-government?

3. What would be dangerous about a prophecy that suggested you should not tell anyone else about it?

4. Both the content and the _____ should be consistent with biblical truth.

THE PLAN, PART ONE:

The Time of Your Life

In the first chapter we discussed that we needed to view prophecy in the larger picture of every believer hearing from God. Now as we move into applying prophecy, we must move from considering that paradigm to seeing your life as the larger picture into which your prophecy must find its place and fit. Jeremiah 21:11 declares that God has a plan for your life. That means that every prophecy God speaks to you will be part of the larger plan He has for you. Therefore, we can say that usually a prophecy is not going to cut right across the middle of the path your life is on, but can be expected to fit into the larger picture of what is going on in your life.

THE RANDOM CHAOS THEORY

Those who do not acknowledge God as the creator of the universe often arrive at the conclusion that all that exists is the byproduct of some accident. They may propose different theories, but all they can ever end up with is random chaos. In other words, they cannot believe there was any plan behind their lives. We who believe in the Divine Creator, by contrast, believe that there was, is, and will be a plan for whatever happens. With this in mind, we understand that if your life is already on the path God has planned for you, a prophecy may bring adjustments and change, but should never bring chaos to your life. It may not be immediately obvious just how a prophecy fits, but given close examination and time, it will. In this chapter we are going to look at how you must see all prophecy through the viewfinder of your own life. This is the first step in developing a plan.

We have talked in earlier chapters about the difficulty in

interpreting time references in prophecy. Now I want to add another important factor in figuring out the timing of a prophecy—*you*. This is your life! God is speaking into it, but your preparedness is still the most important factor when determining timing.

CHARACTER

We must remember that God is always interested in your character as well as your actions. He wants you to do all that you do with integrity. Notice that I did not say that He expects you to do everything perfectly, but that He wants us to walk in integrity. This becomes an important factor in determining how to make a plan for responding to a prophecy. You must be sure you see our own life clearly and how you can respond to any prophecy with integrity.

A CALL AND A CONTRACT

My wife and I received a phone call one evening from some close friends who we really trust. They were heading up a team that was going to Afghanistan with the specific purpose of touching marriages. Although there were nine people signed up to take this trip with them in three different shifts, there was not a single couple signed up to go with them. They called us to say that in their prayer times they believed that

God had spoken to them that we were supposed to go. They were asking us to come to Afghanistan for a month. The hitch in this request was that they were leaving in ten days and would like to have our decision before they left.

Their invitation had to be considered a prophetic invitation. Would this throw us into chaos? It might have, except that we understood the things included in this chapter and immediately began to methodically seek to find if this fit into God's larger plan in our life.

Let me begin the story of our search by stating that we already believed that God wanted us to go to Afghanistan sometime. There had been a couple of discussions about me going previously, and God had recently sparked a desire in my wife to go also. So this invitation was not a complete surprise, but how could we make such a significant decision both confidently and quickly?

After discussion and prayer, we began to lay out in our minds the circumstances in our life that would have to fall in place before we could make a positive response to this prophetic invitation with integrity. The most obvious hurdle was that we had a contract with a medical clinic that we did work for that stipulated a turnaround time on the service we provided for them. It had been difficult to leave town for more than a few days at a time over the previous ten years that we had been doing this work. At this same time, there were serious contract negotiations going on that could adversely affect our future relationship with this source of income. It was already a difficult situation, and then this prophetic invitation was thrown in the middle of it. Still it was clear, we had a contract and integrity demanded that we honor that first before we could respond to the prophetic invitation.

Our relationship with the person who oversaw our contract had always been good, but was usually formal and businesslike. Inquiries to her office usually got a response within a few days to a week. My wife sent an e-mail around nine in the morning explaining the opportunity that had presented itself to us but clearly stated that we, as always, knew our contractual relationship with them was a commitment we must honor. She also stated that we did not want to do anything at this time that would tarnish our good history of service to them or interfere with our future relationship. That same morning, before noon, we had a response that went something like this: "An opportunity like this would never interfere with our future relationship. We will get someone to cover your work for you. Don't worry, just go, be safe, and we will pray for you!" This response was so different from any previous communication we had ever had with this person. We had a clear way to respond to the prophetic invitation in integrity. The rest of the plans for that trip came together smoothly and it was a wonderful experience.

BE HONEST WITH YOURSELF

It is not always as easy as the situation I just shared. Sometimes it requires a much more difficult inspection of your life. As an example, if you received a prophecy about a future ministry, it would require you to ask yourself some serious questions. How prepared am I for this right now? Do I have obligations that integrity demands I take care of first, such as debt? Do I need specific training before I could perform well in this ministry? Do I have the maturity and character to handle the pressure that would accompany this new responsibility? Is there some specific area of weakness in my life that might crumble under the increased pressure if I acted on this prophecy now? All of these questions are really about the same thing, integrity. You would really need to be honest with yourself.

Remember, this is prophecy we are discussing. We have said previously that God often speaks about what is not, as though it were. It does not always have to be done today. If you are not ready now, God has a plan for you to be trained, developed, mentored, prepared, and then released so that you can walk out prophecy with integrity. The best response to a particular prophecy might be to develop a plan on how to prepare yourself. It could involve training. It might include counseling, deliverance, and developing discipline in certain areas of your life. The best plan could well involve serving another person who is already involved in the area God is calling you to. All of these would be excellent responses to a prophecy about a future ministry.

COOPERATING WITH PROPHECY

You always have three choices about how you can respond to prophecy. You can ignore it, resist it, or cooperate with it. I think it is obvious that cooperation is the preferred response. The problem is, that can be harder than it sounds sometimes.

I said earlier that I would go into more detail about the prophetic encounter I had years ago when God said that He was going to hide me for a time because neither the church nor I was ready for the ministry He had for me (I was a pastor at the time). I had no idea what that meant or how I was supposed to respond. No one I talked to was able to help me much, either. So I went about my life with the same zeal that has always been a part of who I am and repeatedly experienced closed doors to anything I tried to do to "serve God."

Finally, I found myself in an isolated rural community where God blessed my involvement in ministries outside the normal church arena. My wife and I spent several years ministering to hardcore outlaw bikers and the homeless. God's hand was with us and on us in these efforts. Even during those years, nothing I ever did inside the church produced much.

Then about six months ago, after I had moved to be nearer my apostolic overseer, I received a prophecy that said something like, "I have kept you hidden but it is almost time for you to become visible." It had been nearly 15 years since I had been told He was going to hide me.

As you can imagine, I was so excited. On the way home from that meeting I was praying, "Now that I am almost ready, what can I do to cooperate?" I thought my response indicated I had learned something in 15 years. God's response was, "Repent." I was not about to be a smart aleck at that moment, but I honestly did not know what He was talking about, so I asked, "For what?" He said, "I told you 15 years ago that I was going to hide you. You have been one of the most difficult people to hide I have ever known." Considering how many people He has known, I knew I had really blown it. It is truly a good thing He is so gracious. Right then, I began to see the last 15 years of my life in a whole new light. He had not been resisting me. He had been hiding me. People had not let me down. He had been hiding me. I was not a failure. He had been hiding me. On and on it went, until I was truly able to repent.

GET SOME HELP

There is a purpose to telling this story. First, I am so glad times have changed and the church is coming into such a better understanding of all things prophetic. When this happened to me, even though I tried, there was no one who could help me understand this prophecy or what I should do about it. I believe that would be different today. If you have prophecies you just do not know how to respond to, get some help from someone who is more experienced than you are. There are those who can counsel you as you develop a plan for response to difficult prophecies.

Second, in Second Corinthians 8 it says that if we are acting out of a willing mind, He is gracious enough to count what we have and not what we lack. I am so glad He lets us make some mistakes without disqualifying ourselves. So do not get under condemnation as you try to figure these things out. Keep going. If you need to, He will show up and give you a chance to repent like He did for me.

Third, do you think my story might have turned out differently if I had known how to cooperate with what God was trying to do in my life? Although it would be a waste of time to speculate about what might have been, I am certain it would have been better if I had known how to cooperate at the beginning of the process as well as at the end. Cooperation really is the preferred response.

So I conclude this section with two encouragements that I have already used as headings: Be honest with yourself and get some help.

CONSIDER YOUR FAMILY

All of our comments thus far have been directed toward you and how your personal life affects the time frame of prophecy.

If you are married, you must also consider how the fulfillment of a prophecy will affect your family. Although we can recite the order of priorities in life as God first, family second, job third, and then ministry, it is very easy to overlook family when it comes to responding to a visionary prophecy. All of the criteria we have reviewed (integrity, character, increased pressure, and preparation) apply to your family as well. Can your marriage handle with integrity what the prophecy presents? Incidentally, integrity in its most basic form means *unity*. Can your spouse handle it? If you have children, how will it affect them, and can they handle the increased pressure? Will the added stress require something of you as parents that you do not currently have the skills or experience to provide? It is not integrity to respond to a prophecy without considering the effect it will have on your family. I am not saying your family will never have to make sacrifices. I am saying you should not put them in a situation they cannot handle with integrity.

Having said all of this, let me add that God will call you to things that are beyond you. Nevertheless, you must consider your family's life and your life as you make a plan for the response to a prophecy about your future.

CHAPTER EIGHT

1. What is the difference between a prophecy bringing change to your life versus it bringing chaos?

2. Explain how the understanding that God wants us to do all things with integrity must be considered when deciding how to respond to a prophecy.

3. To whom might you go to get help with a prophecy that you do not know how to process?

4. How does consideration for your family play a part in laying a plan to cooperate with prophecy?

THE PLAN, PART TWO:

Warring for Your Word

Let's use our imaginations for a minute. Let's pretend your name is Joshua. You have just been made the new leader of a nation. Although that might sound exciting, you must understand that this particular group has a rather bad track record of how it has followed its leader over the past few years. In fact, its former leader was a friend of yours. You know the stress he felt trying to lead this stubborn group and how they questioned every move he made. That takes a little luster off of this new position.

But you are a survivor. You have survived the last 40 years. In fact, you are one of only two adult survivors. "How did you do it?" the reporters ask. You get a distant look in your eyes and the hint of a smile on your face as you talk about your faith in your mighty God. Your confidence surges as you speak of this, because God has promised to be with you just like he was with your predecessor. That helps!

It also helps that you just managed to follow God's instructions and get the whole nation across a swollen river at flood stage without so much as a single damp sock. It seems like it is going pretty well so far. You have had a great ceremony thanking God for the crossing. But you know this people very well. There are things going on that could cause uproar at any minute. They have always had food provided for them by God. It just stopped, and they are going to have to find food on their own. There will probably be some who will complain.

Then there is this whole impending war. You have come into this land to take it away from its current inhabitants. You go out to look at the first city you will attack. This could seem daunting to you. Your troops, while they have had a few battles, are not exactly experienced warriors, and they do not come from a line of very disciplined ancestors. But God is there to encourage you again.

As you head out to look at the city, you are met by a messenger of God to encourage you. Once again, things seem to be in place in your mind. Then God speaks to you. It is always such a pleasure when He does that. He says, "See, I have given Jericho into your hand, with its king *and* the valiant warriors." When you look up, do you know what you will see? You will see a well-fortified city with very high, thick walls with every gate closed and secured. Furthermore, God just said it was full of valiant warriors. Funny, it doesn't look like it has just been given to you. Yet that is what God just said. Right now your attitude is everything. It will determine the outcome.

WHAT'S THE POINT?

All right, back to the present. Even though you are you again and not pretending to be Joshua, that uneasy feeling remains. Frankly, it is a familiar feeling isn't it? Often when God says, "Look what I have given you," we raise our eyes to gaze at something that seems like it is anything but ours. It is often fortified with huge obstacles. It often looks like it belongs to someone else, someone who does not appear agreeable to giving it up. It looks impossible! Furthermore, it is usually filled with valiant warriors, warriors who are way more experienced than we are. At that moment, your attitude is everything. It will determine the outcome.

If we are going to see the fulfillment of our personal prophecies come to pass, we need to look at our attitudes. We have paralleled a medical report throughout this book. The parallel can be helpful here once again. When a patient is faced with seemingly impossible odds, attitude is everything. It may very well be more important than the treatment plan. So while this book will help you develop a plan, your attitudes will have a lot to do with your success in seeing your prophecies come to pass.

LIVING IN A WAR ZONE

We are living in a time of war. It is somewhat confusing to most of us. It is not a very clear-cut war. What are we fighting about? It is an ideological war, not a war for land. Most of us are not very comfortable with it. Yet as Christians we should be used to war. Some of you may be startled by that last statement, but the Bible makes it clear that we are involved in a war over the dominion of the cosmos and ultimately God's authority. You may not be any more comfortable with this truth than you are with our current war with Iraq, but your discomfort does not change it. We need an attitude shift.

No one in Baghdad had the option of waking up this

morning and thinking to himself or herself, "I'm tired of this nonsense. I am not going to be in the middle of a war today." They live in the middle of a war zone whether they feel like it or not. The same is true for every Christian. We live in the middle of a battle zone every day. There is an enemy that does not want your prophecies to come to pass. He has them walled in and the gates are shut with valiant warriors trying to block your access. So what is your attitude going to be? Are you ready to war for your prophetic words?

A WORD TO THE LADIES

Perhaps some of you ladies reading this right now are uncertain you are warriors at all. Let's settle that question right now before we move on. If your children are being threatened by a 75-pound dog or a 250-pound man, you instantly become a 120-pound warrior on wheels. I mean, nobody in their right mind wants to mess with you at that moment. You see, love is a warrior, or as my wife puts it, "The heart of love is the heart of a fighter." So just lay aside the fear that you are not a warrior. One of the things God has called us to be is warriors, and he does not call us without equipping us for the job. You may not be really familiar with that side of yourself that is a warrior. You may have even been discouraged from displaying it, taught that it was not a good thing, that is was wrong, but it is in you.

Twice in the New Testament God is called the *Lord of Sabaoth*. There may be some debate about how to translate that word (note that it is not translated) but in its Hebrew origin it is clearly the feminine form of the word "army." Is God saying he is the Lord of an army of women? Go back to the comment about a 120-pound warrior on wheels. What an army that would be! Every time I think about that, I know that is one army I want to fight along side of. You just need to get a hold of that, ladies, so that you can move ahead in the fulfillment of what God has for you.

VICTORY!

I do not believe you will have victory in any area of life without a warrior's heart. This does not just apply to seeing the fulfillment of your personal prophecies; it applies to every area. So find the warrior within. That does not change the daunting task that seems to be in front of us at the moment God says, "Look what I've given you." It still seems impossible even after you have figured out that there is indeed a warrior in each of us. But if we look up at that walled city as a warrior, we will share the attitude that Joshua had at that moment. We will share his faith in a mighty God. We will have overcome the biggest obstacle that usually lies between us and God's purposes for our lives—ourselves. We will be on the track to victory.

ANOTHER LESSON FROM JOSHUA

Have you noticed that Joshua did not lead the people of Israel to just march around every city until the walls fell down, as they did at Jericho? That would have been so much easier. However, God's strategy for taking each city was different. God does not operate on formulas. Faith and obedience would not mean quite the same thing if we just had to repeat formulas over and over. So even though this book is a practical guide, it is not a formula. What is needed most for your personal prophecies to come to pass is a well-equipped *you* with the right attitude.

JUST DO IT

There is one other aspect of attitude that we must take a closer look at. We are going to return to our medical model to do that. Let's assume that you have given the doctor a thorough explanation of your symptoms; he or she has used all of the best medical tests available to get a clear objective analysis of your problems, which has led to a clear diagnosis for which there is an obvious treatment plan that offers certain cure. That solves everything, right? Unfortunately, it does not. There are people every day who have that kind of clear analysis of their medical problems and yet they never get better because they do not follow through. They don't take their meds. They don't get exercise. They don't lose those extra pounds. To be successful, you just have to do it. Going through the best medical analysis you can get will not be successful unless you *do it!*

It is the same with your personal prophecies. Reading this book will not guarantee that they will be fulfilled. Even memorizing this book from cover to cover will do you no good. What will allow your personal prophecies to come to pass is finding that warrior's heart within you and just doing it. The subtitle of the next chapter is *Initiating the Plan.* Are you ready? Good—so let's just do it!

CHAPTER NINE

—◁ⅈ▷—

1. Honestly, how would you have felt had you been Joshua standing there looking at Jericho?

2. Can you describe a similar event in your life when God said he had given you something that seemed impossible?

3. Do you see yourself as living in a war zone?

4. Do you see yourself as having a warrior's heart?

THE PLAN, PART THREE:

Initiating the Plan

S o your prophecy has passed all the tests, you have run it through all the parameters, and you believe it is the voice of God to you. For some of you, it may be a recent prophecy. For many of you it is a prophecy, or even a series of prophecies, that was given over a period of time but has not yet come to pass. You have probably to some degree hung your hope for the future on these prophecies. Consequently, if they did not come to pass as quickly as you may have expected, your disappointment may be connected to them as well. What should you do? How do you responsibly fulfill your part of causing the word to come to pass? Have you searched within yourself and discovered a warrior's heart to press on? Are you ready to initiate a plan?

Mix It with Faith

If we are going to see the fulfillment of prophecy in our life, one thing is certain. We must learn how to mix the prophecy with faith. Hebrews 4:2b says, "but the message they heard was of no value to them, because those who heard did not combine it with faith" (NIV). We certainly do not want that to happen to us. So we need to make sure we combine our prophecies with faith. That sounds easy—well, maybe not easy. How do you properly mix faith and your prophecy?

I received incredibly wonderful teaching when I was younger from my mentors. As I have grown older, my appreciation for that has deepened. *But...* There was one teaching that I now believe was detrimental to my development towards God's plan for my life. I was taught that to do anything in response to prophetic words spoken over you was to take the responsibility solely in your own hands and cause them to be "self-fulfilled." Nobody would want to do that! That would be strife. The things that God had spoken to me were so impossible that there was no way I could ever have caused them to happen anyway. So I waited and waited and waited and waited. Every once in a while, I would do something to try to help the process along and then feel guilty for having done so. I was sure my efforts reflected negatively on my faith.

Then one Saturday morning, as my wife slept beside me, I had an extended conversation with God about my frustration, disappointment, and confusion in regards to the progress of my life. As I ended my prayer, I reached over to my nightstand and retrieved a magazine to read. As I opened it, my eyes fell on a quote. It read, "If you wait, all you will get is older." The voice of God was speaking to me through this secular magazine. That morning, I began my search to understand what I should do to fulfill my responsibility to respond correctly to prophecy.

TWO EXTREMES

Before we continue, I want us to look at two extremes as a precautionary measure to keep us in balance. I once heard a man who is now an international leader give a testimony about an incident that happened while he was a young, penniless minister. He was standing on a street corner in a southern California city when he felt God was telling him that he was to fly to some city in the eastern United States. He responded by telling God he was willing to go but the airfare would cost $200, and he had nothing. He then felt that he heard the voice of God say, "Look under your right shoe." When he lifted his foot on that street corner, there was a one hundred dollar bill under his shoe. He responded by thanking God but reminding Him that this was only half enough. Then God said, "Look under your left shoe." You can guess what the rest of the story was.

This was an extraordinary experience that most of us will never duplicate. We all wish we could have such an exciting fulfillment to a prophecy, but we must recognize that this story represents one extreme.

I heard another story about a married man with a family who received a prophecy that he was going to go to Africa as a missionary. This man, believing he should act on what was said, sold his car, bought an airline ticket, quit his job, left his family, and flew to Africa. He returned a short time later to a crumbling marriage, without a job or a car, and without having accomplished anything in Africa. Needless to say, he was disillusioned and confused. This was a case of *self-fulfilling* a prophecy. It represents the other extreme.

FAITH DEMANDS ACTION

I have presented you with three possibilities. Most of us will never find hundred-dollar bills under our shoes. None of us wants to repeat the man's trip to Africa. Neither do we want to wait and just grow older. While entering into strife to attempt to self-fulfill a prophecy is not an expression of faith, doing nothing is just as bad. Faith demands action!

James 2:18 says, "But someone will say, 'You have faith; I have deeds.' Show me your faith without deeds, and I will show you my faith by what I do." (NIV) Somewhere between self-fulfilling strife and doing nothing, there is an appropriate, faith-induced response.

EZEKIEL 37

In the first 14 verses of Ezekiel 37, I believe there is a pattern for how we can respond to prophecy. In these verses, God gives Ezekiel instructions on how to bring a prophetic act to completion. I believe we can learn how to combine faith with our prophecies as we apply the model given here.

> *The hand of the Lord was upon me, and he brought me out by the Spirit of the Lord and set me in the middle of a valley; it was full of bones. He led me back and forth among them, and I saw a great many bones on the floor of the valley, bones that were very dry. He asked me, "Son of man, can these bones live?" I said, "O Sovereign LORD, you alone know"* (Ezekiel 37:1-3 NIV).

In these first three verses we have a scene where God takes Ezekiel to a valley covered with dry bones. Picture such an experience and realize that this was not a pleasant place. It was a place of death and carnage. There was not a pile of bones in this valley. They were scattered everywhere. It was as though a great battle had been lost here and then the scavengers had come and fed on the bodies of the warriors, scattering their cleanly picked bones across the valley floor. It was not a place for a Sunday afternoon picnic.

IMPOSSIBLE CIRCUMSTANCES

As we saw in the last chapter, prophecy often comes from God right in the middle of overwhelmingly impossible circumstances. Notice, also, that by the Spirit, God brought Ezekiel to this miserable place. Over the last few years we have been singing a lot of songs about rivers. One day I sensed the Lord speak to me and ask if I had ever considered that the rivers run in the lowest places in the valley. We always want to go to the mountain of God, but sometimes He takes us to the low places to accomplish His purposes. That last word is important: *purposes*. God does not bring us to miserable places without a reason. We will discover why He does this as we proceed.

God did not just take Ezekiel there to look at this valley. He made him walk around in the middle of it all. As Ezekiel passed among all these disjointed skeletons, he observed that they were very dry. I believe that is a way of saying that they were very, very dead. I also believe that these human bones were intended to represent human failure. Human effort always leads to human failure and a lot of very dry bones.

Am I talking to the right people? Have you received prophecies in the middle of impossible circumstances? Have you received prophecies only to find yourself being forced to walk in the middle of human failure? Why would God take you to such a place and ask you to do such a thing?

GOD ASKS THE QUESTION

Set your questions aside for a minute because God has a question for Ezekiel. God asks Ezekiel if there is any hope of life in this place. Why does God ask Ezekiel a question? Is it because God did not know the answer? Whenever God asks a question, we had better pay attention. He is not asking because He needs information from us. He asks us questions to move us from where we are to some new place. He asked Ezekiel a question because he was trying to move Ezekiel from hope in human effort to hope in the divine.

Have you gone through circumstances since you received your prophecy that have been discouraging? Perhaps they have even caused you to lose hope. Do not come under condemnation! You may have needed to lose that hope. Perhaps you needed to lose hope in anything human and transfer your hope to God. If circumstances caused you to lose hope, then you need to stop now and confess that to God. You need to reestablish your hope in Him. He, not the devil, took you through those miserable circumstances to get your hope moved solidly to Him.

> *Then he said to me, "Prophesy to these bones and say to them, 'Dry bones, hear the word of the Lord! This is what the Sovereign Lord says to these bones: I will make breath enter you, and you will come to life. I will attach tendons to you and make flesh come upon you and cover you with skin; I will put breath in you, and you will come to life. Then you will know that I am the LORD.'" So I prophesied as I was commanded. And as I was prophesying, there was a noise, a rattling sound, and the bones came together, bone to bone. I looked, and tendons and flesh appeared on them and skin covered them, but there was no breath in them (Ezekiel 37:4-8 NIV).*

RELEASING GOD'S POWER

Once God has established Ezekiel's faith in the divine, He states His method for releasing His power in the earth realm. His creative power has always been released through the spoken word. He spoke the world into existence. When He needed to redeem it, He sent the Word, Jesus. So He had Ezekiel speak all that He had in mind for these bones to them. Today, His creative power is still released through the spoken word i.e. prophecy, confessions of faith, and declarations.

Declaring what God has previously spoken to you through prophecy to the dry bone circumstances you find yourself in is exercising your faith. It is not strife; it is faith. It is not just sitting and waiting; it is proactive. It is not self-fulfilling; it is putting your faith in God to work.

IT'S PROGRESSIVE

Notice that God had a complete plan for these bones. He had a complete plan from A to Z. It started with putting them back together, moved on to putting flesh on them, continued with giving them breath, and concluded with having them arise as a great army once again. But…it did not all happen the first time Ezekiel opened his mouth and prophesied. It did not all manifest immediately. It was progressive.

The first thing that takes place is that each bone comes together with its corresponding bone. You can't just throw bones together randomly and expect to get a functional body. Sing along: "The thigh bone is connected to the leg bone." I am trying to get you to smile because I have experienced that people receive profound truth better when they are smiling than when they are frowning.

PLACEMENT AND STRUCTURE

The coming together of the bones into a skeleton represents two things. For the body to function, there must be proper placement and structure. If within your own natural body your bones were not placed properly, you would be deformed and nonfunctional. A nose growing anyplace other than the middle of your face could not smell and could just look a little funny, too. Furthermore, if you did not have a skeletal structure, you would be a heap of tissue on the floor.

For you to see your prophecies fulfilled and for you to come into your destiny, you need to be correctly placed in the body. Do you know who is over you, under you, and beside you? Do you know your place in the body? Do you know who you are connected to?

That brings us to the second point: structure. There is a structural framework that must exist in the Body of Christ in order for it to be functional. That is true for the body as a whole and each member of it. If you want to see the prophecies in your life come to fulfillment, you need to be a connected part of the structural government in a local church. Are you still smiling? I hope so, because our destinies are all tied together as a body.

FLESHING IT OUT

The next thing that happened after Ezekiel declared the word of the Lord to these dry circumstances is that tendons and muscles and skin begin to cover the skeletons. In our natural bodies, this flesh accomplishes two purposes. The first thing is that they simply hold our body parts together.

I recently had to have a total knee replacement due to a motorcycle accident 28 years ago. It became very clear to me after the surgery that there are not pivot pins in our joints like there are in door hinges that hold the two parts together. There really is nothing holding your knee joint together but your tendons and muscles. If those tendons and muscles are not strong, your knee joint is not strong. The structure of my knee is now made of steel and plastic that are probably stronger that the original bone, but I had to work very hard to rebuild the muscles and tendons to stabilize the knee and make it useful.

Proper placement in the structure of the Body of Christ does little good if there is not something that binds us there. Commitment! Covenant! That is not the only thing that binds us together—just the most courageous. I would not be committed where I did not have love and relationship. The three—love, relationship, and covenant—go together like tendons, muscles, and skin. That is the kind of environment where you can have hope restored to fulfill your destiny.

The second thing that our tendons, muscles, and skin allow our bodies to do is perform work. That skeleton hanging in your doctor's office cannot accomplish any task. Our muscles, when properly attached to tendons and contained by our skin, allow us to accomplish the work of walking, lifting, and even punching computer keys, as I am doing now. So they represent to us the equipping of the saints for the work of the ministry (Eph. 4). You need to be a committed, properly placed member of a local fellowship so you can be equipped. Going through this process is part of what you need to do to express faith in the future that God has spoken of to you.

"YOU ARE LIKE JOSEPH"

Once when my wife and I were in a situation where our gifts were not being accepted, we needed to know how to behave in some practical situations. The Lord spoke to my wife in her heart and said, "You are like Joseph." When we sat down and tried to figure out what this meant, it was obvious that on his way to being his family's deliverer, Joseph found himself in at least three different places where his true calling was not wholly recognized. Those were in his own family, in

Potipher's house as a slave, and in prison. Joseph did not let other's failure to see him as he was called to be keep him from being who he was. Eventually, through his faithfulness to the revelation he had about himself, he did find his way into his destiny.

So as you wait for the full manifestation of the things that have been spoken to you through prophecies, just do whatever you find in front of you that you can. Just be who you are where you are. This is an excellent way to express the faith you are mixing with the prophecies you have received.

> *Then he said to me, "Prophesy to the breath; prophesy, son of man, and say to it, 'This is what the Sovereign Lord says: Come from the four winds, O breath, and breathe into these slain, that they may live.'" So I prophesied as he commanded me, and breath entered them; they came to life and stood up on their feet—a vast army* (Ezeikel 37:9-10 NIV).

DECLARE IT AGAIN

In verses 9 and 10 we learn that Ezekiel now had a whole army of normal-looking people standing in front of him that were still dead. There was still no breath in them. Some might consider that worse than standing in a valley full of dry bones. Ezekiel was not discouraged. In obedience he declared the plan of God again.

God instructed Ezekiel to call the breath out of the four winds. Note that the breath was not the four winds, it was just amongst them. I believe as we make personal application of these verses that the breath is the Holy Spirit. The Holy Spirit is out there moving throughout the four corners of the earth. There comes a time when we are properly placed, properly connected, and properly equipped, and then we must find the faith to call on the Spirit to come from the four corners and fall on us.

I think that we have done this often without meeting the three requirements mentioned in the previous sentence and wondered why it did not work. Can you see how, when you have met those requirements and know you are truly ready, you will have confidence to call, "Spirit come, for I am prepared!" Wow, I get goosebumps just writing it.

STANDING FIRM

As Ezekiel called and the breath came, the bodies were filled, and they stood at attention. My mind may work in odd ways, but as I read this, I wondered what were the bodies doing before? Sitting? Slouching? Or even lying down? How are you doing with the prophecies you have for your future? Are you standing firm? Or have you begun to slouch as time has passed? Some of you may have become so discouraged that you have sat down. Don't give up! You can still stir up your faith and get up. You can reenter the process. It's not too late.

I love to read the last half of Ephesians 6:13 and the first part of verse 14 together: "...and after you have done everything, to stand. Stand firm then..." (NIV). If you want to see the fulfillment of those prophetic words, you have to do what you need to do, and then stand firm.

> *Then he said to me: "Son of man, these bones are the whole house of Israel. They say, 'Our bones are dried up and our hope is gone; we are cut off.' Therefore prophesy and say to them: 'This is what the Sovereign Lord says: O my people, I am going to open your graves and bring you up from them; I will bring you back to the land of Israel (Ezekiel 37:11-12).*

HOPE DEFERRED

The bones have been properly placed. They have been connected. They are equipped. The breath has come into them, but the job is still not complete. Verses 11 and 12 tell us that they are still dried up, hopeless, and cut off.

Hope deferred makes you sick and dried up. Proverbs 13:12-13 says, "Hope deferred makes the heart sick, but desire fulfilled is a tree of life. The one who despises the word will be in debt to it, but the one who fears the commandment will be rewarded." We have always assumed that the consequences of "hope deferred" were all negative. Is it possible that waiting is also part of the process to determine if we will stand firm in our prophecies or if we will become sick of the wait and reject them?

I must confess that there have been moments when I have gone to God and said things like, "Why did You ever say that to me if it is not going to come to pass? It would have been better to have never heard it." I struggled my way through those dark moments and always ended up concluding, "Since You are God, I have no choice but to go on believing You."

Proverbs 13:13 says that even when you despise those unfulfilled words, you are still tied to them. The solution to disappointment is not in rejecting them but in clinging to the fear of the Lord.

RECONNECT WITH YOUR INHERITANCE

Not only were Ezekiel's recently resurrected soldiers dried up and sick, they were also cut off. This refers to their inheritance. They were cut off from their inheritance. Are those unfulfilled prophecies promises of your inheritance and of your destiny? If you do not have a hold on them yet, keep prophesying. Keep proclaiming. God says He will bring you out of your grave and into your inheritance!

WHY SO LONG?

Why is this such a long drawn out process? Some of you may be thinking that it is hardly worth it. Is there a purpose in all of this? Absolutely!

> *"Then you, my people, will know that I am the Lord, when I open your graves and bring you up from them. I will put my Spirit in you and you will live, and I will settle you in your own land. Then you will know that I the Lord have spoken, and I have done it, declares the Lord"* (Eziekel 37: 13-14 NIV).

WHO DID THAT?

Verses 13 and 14 tell answer the question, "Why so long?" It is so you will know who did all of this in our life. You will know that God did it, that you are His child, and that you have come into your inheritance. He does not want you to have any question in regards to any of those three things. He is your Father. You are His child. He has brought you into your inheritance. It is worth the wait and the effort.

REVIEWING THESE STEPS

- **STEP ONE:** Recognize those difficult circumstances as the perfect place for God to demonstrate His power in your life.

- **STEP TWO:** Mix faith with your prophecy. Make sure your faith and hope are in God, not human efforts.

- **STEP THREE:** Put your faith in action and speak the prophecy you have received to the dry circumstances you find yourself in. This is proactive faith.

- **STEP FOUR:** Make sure you know your place in a functional body of believers. This is where you will learn to operate as you are supposed to and find the path to your destiny. This allows all that God has spoken to you to come to pass.

- **STEP FIVE:** Get in a body of believers where you can experience love, relationship, and commitment as you are equipped for your future.

+ STEP SIX: When you are properly placed, properly connected, and properly equipped, call on the Holy Spirit to come and give life to your prophecies. Declare them again!

+ STEP SEVEN: Stand firm!

+ STEP EIGHT: Set aside any sickness caused by the waiting and keep claiming your inheritance.

+ STEP NINE: When you have received the fulfillment of your prophecy, the final step is to thank Him!

IDENTIFY YOURSELF

You need to identify your current location in this process. Some of you may have stopped having faith in your word. Perhaps you have even despised it. If you have bailed out of the process, confess it to the Father, repent, and get back in the process.

Others of you can see yourselves along the way. There are two things you should do. Keep proclaiming by faith to your present circumstances that God is faithful, cooperating in whatever stage of this process you find yourself. Second, review each stage and see if you have missed any or are weak in any, and work on those areas also.

FINAL WORDS

I believe we can summarize the lessons of Ezekiel 37 in two words—declare and prepare. To declare the prophetic vision that God has given you to your circumstances and to prepare yourself for the ultimate fulfillment of those words are both acts of faith. My final words to you are, keep the faith and don't quit until you see the fulfillment of your prophecies.

God bless you on your journey as you move toward your fulfilled prophecies, your destiny, and your inheritance.

CHAPTER TEN

1. How does the author's illustration of reading the statement, "If you wait, all you will get is older," fit with mixing faith with our prophecies?

2. While not wanting to be involved in self-fulfillment of prophecy, faith demands _____.

3. How does the impossibility of the circumstances play a role in helping us decide on the legitimacy of a prophecy?

4. How does the story in Ezekiel 37 illustrate that the fulfillment of a prophecy may be progressive?

5. Do you have any prophecies in your life where hope has been deferred? If so, how can you reconnect with your inheritance?

PROPHETIC NOTES

For more information about
MORE THAN WORDS MINISTRIES, INC.,
the services we offer, and other products,
contact us at:

info@mtwm.org.

Website: www.mtwm.org.